BEST BEFORE

Written by

Heather Grace Stewart

Logline:

When thousands of Americans receive texts six months after they were sent, three women's love lives fall apart in heartbreaking and hilarious ways before they can help each other find their way again.

Book 5 - LOVE AGAIN SERIES

WGA Registered #2117704

Heather Grace Stewart

Best Before

A Screenplay

Published by Graceful Publications, November 2021

NOTE: This romcom screenplay is 85 pages long as a Final Draft file, but to accommodate the spine of the paperback book and to ease your reading, the book has a wider left margin, the font size is 16, and at times I've left some longer spaces between scenes. Therefore, the book version runs longer.

Special thanks for the kind help, advice, and your time: Bill, Kayla, Blake Snyder and his

Save The Cat! book, Aaron Sorkin and Masterclass, Editor Peter Carter, Author Evie Alexander, Author Cassidy Reyne, George Shirreff, Editor Jennifer Bogart, Stephanie Dean-Patterson, Arianna Merritt, Natalie Wolicki, ISU Emerging Screenwriters Competition, Blue Cat Screenplay Competition, Write LA, Taleflick Productions.

To read more books by bestselling Amazon author Heather Grace Stewart, please visit her official website, heathergracestewart.com or visit **Shor.by/HGS**

Sign up with one click for her Readers Club, to be entered in her contests and to learn first about her exclusive book bargains and new releases.

STRANGELY,INCREDIBLY GOOD SERIES:

Strangely, Incredibly Good

Remarkably Great

LOVE AGAIN SERIES:

The Ticket

Good Nights

The Friends I've Never Met (Screenplay format)

Lauren from Last Night

Best Before (Screenplay format)

FOR THE KIDS:

The Groovy Granny

POETRY:

Where the Butterflies Go

Leap!

Carry On Dancing

Three Spaces

Caged: New and Selected Poems

Stargazing

EXT. ATLANTIC BEACH PARK, RHODE ISLAND - **MAY - DAY, 20 YEARS AGO**

A northern gannet's wings open wide as it soars over the North Atlantic Ocean across a clear blue sky.

As the opening song about lasting friendship fades, the gannet lands on the beach. The ocean surf roars onto the sand. People laugh as they ride the Ferris wheel beside the beach. All the bright colors and joyful sounds of a fair on a summer day are amplified across the fairgrounds.

EXT. ATLANTIC BEACH PARK, RHODE ISLAND TILT-A-WHIRL RIDE - MAY - DAY, **20 YEARS AGO**

A gorgeous, exuberant 19-YEAR-OLD CHARLENE (CHARLIE) JAMES is pulling

20-YEAR-OLD DAYTON HILL to their seat on the Tilt-a- Whirl ride. He tries to pull away from the situation, laughing. She shoves him into his seat and puts on his belt for him.

DAYTON

I'm warning you. I'm prone to puking!

CHARLIE

Dayton Hill, track star. I thought you had abs of steel? Don't be such a wuss!

DAYTON

I shouldn't have had that second bacon chili cheese dog.

The ride starts moving. Dayton braces himself. Charlie starts laughing and opens her arms wide to the sky, embracing the joy. Dayton looks down at her lovingly.

DAYTON (CONT'D)

How do you do it?

CHARLIE

Do what?

DAYTON

Approach everything in the world with open

arms.

CHARLIE

I dunno. Because the opposite would be

depressing?

DAYTON

You're fearless.

The ride picks up speed, so CHARLIE has to

shout her response as their bodies are flung

backward against their seat. Even the way she

shouts this seems fearless.

CHARLIE

Nah-uh! I'm afraid of lots of things. But you can
take on anything beside the right person!

DAYTON is moved by her compliment and
love.

DAYTON

Okay, Whirl-a-girl. If I don't do this, I'm going
to regret it for the rest of my life.

CHARLIE

If you don't do what?

DAYTON cradles her face in the palms of his
hands and kisses her passionately. She leans in
and responds the same way. The ride is moving
faster, but they don't notice. They're lost in their
first kiss. After some time, CHARLIE pulls
away, giddy and dizzy.

CHARLIE (CONT'D)

That was...wow. Mind-blowing. Fearless! But puke on me bucko, and it's over.

DAYTON
(yelling above the ride noise)

Never, Charlie. This will never be over.

Their kiss has given him strength. He holds on and grins, enjoying the ride.

EXT. ATLANTIC BEACH PARKING LOT - **LATER THAT DAY**

People are bustling about the fairgrounds, getting on and off rides, buying food, trying to win stuffed toys, enjoying a beautiful day at the park together.

DAYTON and CHARLIE are walking the busy fairgrounds hand in hand, laughing hard over a joke DAYTON has made.

CHARLIE has a huge stuffed penguin in one hand; DAYTON has popcorn in the other. When their laughter subsides, they gaze lovingly at each other. DAYTON's BODYGUARD is behind him, being discreet.

They arrive at the parking lot area. A mob of 20 teen girls rushes off of a tourist bus and runs toward DAYTON. FANGIRL1 waves a poster of DAYTON and his newly famous band. It reads "THE SUMMER SENSATION"

FANGIRL1

Omeegod I can't believe we found you!

BODYGUARD

Step back please.

FANGIRL2 grabs DAYTON's arm, causing him to drop CHARLIE's hand and his popcorn all over the pavement.

CHARLIE

Hey, give him space.

FANGIRL1

Who the hell are you? Move it!

FANGIRL1 hip-checks CHARLIE out of the way. DAYTON reaches for her but can't get to her anymore.

DAYTON

I'm so sorry Charlie, I never imagined!...

FANGIRL2

Sign my boob! Sign my boob!

FANGIRL1

Wait, I was here first!

All the teen girls have circled around DAYTON. CHARLIE stands outside the circle looking forlorn. Her stuffed penguin has been trampled and is lying on the pavement.

A limo squeals to a halt in front of the mob. DAYTON's bodyguard opens the front door and shoves DAYTON inside. As he does so, DAYTON looks over his shoulder at CHARLIE. He catches her eye. He looks miserable.

They speed off, leaving CHARLIE stranded, tears brimming her eyes. The gaggle of girls is hysterical as they compare who touched DAYTON where.

INT. DAYTON'S LIMOUSINE - DAY

DAYTON is trying to see out the back of the limo window, but it's darkened and he can't see anything. He plays with the lock on his door but it makes a clicking sound. He's locked into this life. He knocks hard on the glass partition and it rolls down to reveal his publicist J.J., 45, balding and tired looking, who is seated up front.

J.J.

What is it, kid?

DAYTON

J.J., You have to turn back!

J.J.

We can't go back into that mob. Besides, you
have a show tonight.

DAYTON

I thought you said I could take a night off.

J.J.

Do you want to sell records?

DAYTON

Yea...I guess...

J.J.

You wanna sell records, kid, you're gonna have to play all the cities. From Hong Kong to Saint Louis du Ha- Ha!

DAYTON

Saint Louis du What Now?

J.J.

Never mind kid. You're gonna be playing all over the world!

DAYTON

But, I have a girlfriend now! Charlie.

He sighs as he says her name and dreamily looks out the window.

DAYTON (CONT'D)

And you just left her there!

J.J.

Relax kid, I'll send another car for her, make sure she gets home.

DAYTON

But I don't want to tour the world. I just want to see Charlie again.

J.J.

No girlfriends. It's in your contract!

DAYTON

What? It is not!

J.J.

It practically is. It's what I say is gonna work.

DAYTON

That's not the same, stop the B.S.!

J.J.

Hey hey, no lip, kid. I can make it all go away. All the money, all the fame. Listen to me or lose it. No girlfriends! You gotta keep the girl customers hooked. Got that?

DAYTON didn't see this news coming. He's heartbroken.

DAYTON

I guess...

J.J. doesn't wait to listen for his answer before making the partition window roll back up again.

DAYTON turns away and places the top of his head on his window. He closes his eyes, holding back tears.

INT. CHARLIE'S APARTMENT - DOWNTOWN NEW YORK - VALENTINE'S DAY - **PRESENT DAY**

SUBTITLE: 20 YEARS LATER.

CHARLENE (CHARLIE) JAMES, 39, still good-looking and good- natured, but frazzled, her blonde-grey hair tied up in a messy bun, grabs her cell and keys and prepares to leave her small two-bedroom apartment holding a cumbersome white garment bag. She uses her foot to gently push away a cat that's trying to follow her out the door. Another insistent cat isn't far behind the first one. She puts down the bag and pushes them both back inside.

CHARLIE

Not today, sweet things. You can't come. I'm not playing the crazy old cat lady today.

EXT. STREETS OF NEW YORK, VALENTINE'S DAY - DAY

CHARLIE leaves a café and walks on the sidewalk past busy shops, hoisting the garment bag over her head to avoid hitting people on their way to work.

She now has a tray of three hot chocolates in the other hand. She is juggling the garment bag, slung high over one shoulder, and the tray, but she remains in good spirits and doesn't seem to mind the minor inconvenience. She's the kind of person who laughs at herself.

CHARLIE stops and turns to look into the alley beside the café. JOSH, an unshaven homeless man who looks young, 35, looks up from his sleeping bag and nods at her. He has on a pair of wool gloves but no other warm clothing, and is holding an older model of a phone in one hand. She bends down to him, letting the garment bag fall onto the pavement.

CHARLIE

Josh. Buddy. Why are you back here? Please go to that warming centre I told you about, okay? It's a cold one today.

JOSH closes his eyes but nods in understanding. She hands him a ten- dollar bill from her pocket, then takes one hot chocolate and passes it to him. He acknowledges it with a warm smile, like she has done this before.

JOSH

(mumbles) Charlie. Doll. You take such good care of me. Lost everything. But not you...

She gets up to leave, then changes her mind. She takes the scarf around her neck and gently wraps it around JOSH's neck. She leaves him with the full tray of drinks at his side, takes her bag and continues on her way.

We follow CHARLIE out the alley and around the corner.

EXT - STREET OF NYC - NEXT STREET OVER - VALENTINE'S DAY

Bright, tacky Valentine's decorations adorn every shop window on the street.

A light snowfall leaves its traces on hats and scarves. Some people are checking their phones with baffled looks on their faces.

A few people on both sides of the street stop to gape at their phones, holding up sidewalk traffic. Someone honks at a man in his car, stopped at the stop light because he's staring at his phone and shaking his head in confusion.

After having to stop for the slow-walkers and phone gapers, CHARLIE continues on her way. A woman selling red roses beside a wooden HAPPY VALENTINE'S DAY sign shoves one under CHARLIE's nose. She smiles politely and shakes her head as she moves the woman's hand away from her face and keeps walking.

CHARLIE (V.O.)

When you're a woman nearing 40, society can make you feel like you're walking around with a Best Before date stamped on your forehead. You'd like to think of the growing age lines on your face as treasure maps of where you've been and where you're going, but the last Insta post you saw told you to Face-Tune yourself back to seventeen. The last commercial you saw insisted wrinkles and stretch marks are ugly and unwanted.

INT. NEW YORK BRIDAL SHOP - VALENTINE'S DAY

CUT TO:

CHARLIE walks inside a light and airy bridal shop with expensive looking dresses in the window. She nods and smiles at a SHOP WOMAN who is standing at the cash counter staring at her phone in utter confusion like the people on the streets outside. She puts down her phone when CHARLIE comes closer.

The women greet each other like old friends. CHARLIE hands SHOP WOMAN the garment bag, and the woman unzips it, and takes out what's inside, hanging up a gorgeous silk off-white wedding gown in a change room for

CHARLIE. CHARLIE closes the curtain and starts getting into the strapless dress. We see her face close up, looking at herself in the mirror as she changes. Her eyes and upper lip have small wrinkles that add character to her 39-year-old face. She takes off her glasses to look at herself more closely. She's introspective and malcontent.

CHARLIE (V.O. CONT)

If our bodies, faces and skills have "Best Before" dates, does that mean our lives do, too? The challenge is to believe that there's a Best After date. Despite the messages we're fed daily, to believe that life and love can blossom after 40, and female friendships can be better than ever.

INT. MASTER BEDROOM - NEW YORK TOWNHOUSE - VALENTINE'S DAY

SHARON, 39, curvy with grey-brown hair flowing across her shoulders and bare breasts, is sprawled out like a starfish, stark naked on a bed sprinkled in red and pink rose petals. She's giddy with nervous energy. There are full champagne glasses on both bedside tables.

The front door creeks open downstairs, and there's a beeping sound as someone is turning off the front door alarm.

The double doors to the bedroom open slowly. Sharon adjusts her body on the bed so it's in the most sensuous pose that she can make at her age, but with all of this sprawling, she pulls a lower back muscle. She howls a little, with a British Yorkshire accent.

SHARON

Crikey! Must do more yin.

SHARON rubs her lower back, laughing at herself, and composes herself again for her lover's big entrance.

SHARON (CONT'D)

Darling, I got your text!

FEMALE REAL ESTATE AGENT

And this gorgeous master bedroom has a lovely pair of...

FIVE-YEAR-OLD BOY BROWSING TOWNHOUSE WITH MOTHER

Boobies! Bare boobies!

FEMALE REAL ESTATE AGENT

(Turns away, covers the boy's eyes)

Those aren't supposed to be here.

SHARON

(Covering herself with sheet) Bollocks!

FEMALE REAL ESTATE AGENT

(Shoves Mother and son out of the room and closes one door) What in God's name is this?

SHARON

Afternoon sex, supposedly. With my boyfriend. He texted for me to come home! Who are you?

REAL ESTATE AGENT

Your real estate agent, supposedly. He hired me to sell your home.

SHARON's eyes open wide. Her excitement has turned to horror. She pulls the sheet up higher to her chin, takes the champagne and downs the whole glass in one fell swoop.

SHARON

The wanker was trying to sell our place without even telling me.

INT. FANCY NEW YORK RESTAURANT - VALENTINE'S DAY - NOON

A busy, upscale restaurant with dim lighting and red roses on every table. JUSTINE, 39, gorgeous, African American, hair in braided updo, is sharing a plate of sushi with her partner JERRY, 40. He's on his phone, not paying her any attention, while other couples around them are whispering sweet nothings to one another.

Her phone pings. She looks at the message. She looks at him quizzically.

JUSTINE

Why are you texting me?

JERRY

(looks up) I'm not?

JUSTINE

(holds up her phone to show him) This says you don't love me anymore. That you want...more.

JERRY leans in, reads his wife's phone messages and hesitates, furrowing his brow. He's putting the pieces together. When he finally does, he looks like he is witnessing a horrific traffic accident.

JERRY

Oh my God.

JUSTINE

You asked me for an open marriage during our Valentine's Day lunch?

JERRY puts down his phone and gets up to comfort his wife. It doesn't work. She's getting up to leave. He takes her hand but she struggles to pull away from him.

A WAITRESS has arrived with a tray of two elaborate meals. She moves in to put JUSTINE's plate in front of her, but is rudely pushed aside by JERRY.

JERRY

No! I sent that text to you six months ago. I can't for the life of me figure out why you're getting it now!

The WAITRESS spins around awkwardly, tray in one hand, plate in the other, unsure of what to do next.

JUSTINE

You want us to sleep with other people? To stay married but screw the neighbors?

The WAITRESS raises her eyebrows and backs away from the situation, then quickly walks back to the kitchen.

People in the restaurant are staring at them as they raise their voices. JERRY looks like he's going to vomit. He tries to caress her shoulders, but she squirms away.

JERRY

Justine, Angel pie...Muffin...

JUSTINE rolls her eyes at the pet names.

JUSTINE

What? Just tell me!

JERRY

You texted back 'Fine, whatever.' I thought you already agreed!

JUSTINE

Fuck you to the moon and back. I never agreed to that. This isn't happening.

JUSTINE pulls on her winter coat and storms out of the restaurant, coming back quickly to take the dozen red roses JERRY had given her. She glares at him with murderous intentions.

JUSTINE (CONT'D)

I'm selling these. Probably going to need the money.

She leaves. The WAITRESS returns and plunks both meals down in front of JERRY, gives him a dirty look and walks away. JERRY has his head in his hands and doesn't look like he's very hungry. Everyone in the restaurant is giving him a dirty look.

INT. NEW YORK BRIDAL SHOP - VALENTINE'S DAY

CHARLIE is in her off-white wedding gown, standing on a raised altar. Her younger sister, ALLIE MCCARNEY, is sitting on the sofa watching. CHARLIE's back is facing the large floor to ceiling mirrors. She's looking at her back, which is too snug in the dress, and touching her boobs, which are spilling out of it, and then looking at ALLIE for an opinion, clearly feeling insecure about how it's fitting her back and chest. SHOP WOMAN rushes up to her and spreads the dress out more, then ALLIE touches the front of the dress and lifts it up. CHARLIE lifts half an inch off the floor.

ALLIE

If you hoist it every so often, your girls will stay in better.

CHARLIE

So I'm supposed to walk down the aisle like this?

CHARLIE holds the fabric in front of her breasts, lifting it up on either side, elbows out dramatically. She makes a face. ALLIE wraps her arms around her and the two sisters collapse in laughter.

SHOP WOMAN

For women your age...ample breasts are normal. You've had babies. You can't expect to have a teenager's body in your forties.

CHARLIE is offended.

CHARLIE

I couldn't have any babies and I'm not forty for another month.

ALLIE

Charlie, don't stress. We have one more fitting before your August wedding. You can fix this. You did a gorgeous job of Pete's and my wedding at the farmhouse. Marrying Sterling should be a cakewalk for you.

CHARLIE looks at herself in the mirror, clearly upset about more than how the dress looks.

CHARLIE

I'm not so sure...about anything...

ALLIE

What are you saying?

CHARLIE

Is a second wedding a cakewalk?

Everyone will be either judging or pitying me.

ALLIE doesn't know what to say so she just stands there biting her lower lip. She knows CHARLIE is right.

CHARLIE (CONT'D)

Oh crap, the cake! I haven't ordered my couple's cake!

She puts her hands to her head, stressed out. There's a ping sound, and CHARLIE looks over at a white sofa where her purse lies, her phone on top of it. She jumps off the altar and waddles over to the sofa to sit and look at her phone.

CUT TO:

CLOSE UP OF CHARLIE'S PHONE From: DAYTON HILL

<Charlie, It was so good seeing you again. I think about you all the time. I'll always love you. We should meet.>

BACK TO

CHARLIE reads the text, then looks up at Allie, tears in her eyes, her mouth wide open. She can't hide her shock.

ALLIE

Who is it?

CHARLIE

Murphy and his lame-ass law.

INT. CHARLIE'S APARTMENT, NEW YORK - VALENTINE'S NIGHT

CHARLIE is alone in a living room in near-darkness on a small sofa. She's wearing her off-white wedding dress, her phone in one hand, a glass of red wine in other. She's had half a bottle. She's listening to rock ballad songs on the smart home device beside her. The skirt of her dress is bunched up around her, so she looks like a frosted cupcake, her breasts overflowing, her expression forlorn.

There's a worn-looking stuffed penguin beside her bunched-up skirt that looks exactly like the one Dayton won for her so many years ago, a heart-shaped box of chocolates she's been eating, and a tablet propped up on the coffee table in front of her. She's waiting for it to ring but also staring at the penguin and her phone every two minutes.

STREAMING RADIO DJ (V.O.)
And this legendary rocker's still got it. Here's "When You Were My Girl" by the one and only Dayton Hill. Makes you want to kiss the one you love.

The rock ballad begins like this:

DAYTON
(Singing) Cotton candy kisses, Spinning under the moon, Our sweet story ended, all too soon.

CHARLIE

(Sighs, blowing a hair out of her face) And suddenly he's everywhere. Alexa, turn off the music!

The music stops abruptly. CHARLIE's 24-year-old roommate HARMONY, enters the living room in dark clothes, black lipstick, and a spiked black leather choker, heading for the kitchen. She's muttering dark words and incantations, poking a small doll's eyes with needles.

CHARLIE shudders when she sees what she's doing.

CHARLIE (CONT'D)

Harmony, do you have to do that out here? I told you it gives me the creeps.

HARMONY

Don't do that voodoo that I do so well?

Charlie groans and rolls her eyes. HARMONY starts to chuckle. CHARLIE rubs her forehead, trying to massage away her headache.

CHARLIE

Please just stop. And move those tree trunk stumps!

She looks over to the centre of the room where two polished tree trunk stumps hold a witchcraft book and several plastic skull candles.

HARMONY

They are an ode to the earth. They are my altar.

CHARLIE

Who are you, Greta Thunberg? I didn't sign up for half an old growth forest in my living room!

HARMONY

Why should I move them? I pay half the rent.

She stops pacing and poking the doll and stares at CHARLIE in her dress.

HARMONY (CONT'D)

What are you wearing that for?

CHARLIE

(Looking at her phone again, bites lower lip, flattens her dress bodice) It's helping me make a decision.

HARMONY

Okaaay? Whatever. So, like, this doll is my ex-boyfriend, in case you were wondering. He's getting married. I'm gonna make him hurt so bad he urinates out of his eyeballs.

CHARLIE

(standing) Enough! Enough with the witchcraft or you'll have to move!

HARMONY

(rolls her eyes) Move? Last month you said you needed my rent money. To help pay for the funeral. But you're getting married *again*...

CHARLIE looks gutted when the funeral is mentioned. She has to sit down. Her voice quivers.

CHARLIE

Richard's hospital and funeral costs blind-sided me, yes, because he had no insurance. I'm still paying it off three years later. But last month when you signed the lease you were into Elvis tunes and poodle skirts! You ordered a kit online and turned Wiccan in two weeks! Can't you just do the voodoo in your room?

HARMONY

My room's too small. Witchcraft needs...air. Wind, fire!

HARMONY grins, revealing black lipstick on her front tooth. She pulls a lighter from her pocket, opens her backpack and pulls out plastic white skulls and sage. She places four skulls on the floor, then lights the tip of a bundle of white sage and sweetgrass, and starts pointing it at CHARLIE's forehead.

HARMONY (CONT'D)

You are resistant to change. On some level, you think you're not worthy of better things in your life. Why is that, Charlie?

CHARLIE blinks and takes a step back. She throws her hand up in the air in the STOP motion.

CHARLIE

Oh and you're doing so much better?

HARMONY

I moved here from Canada, in politically uncertain times. I'm all about the change. You. You're basically marrying a carbon copy of your last husband and from what I gather, neither of them made you happy.

CHARLIE is completely taken aback.

CHARLIE

What you gather? From what you GATHER? Have you been listening to my phone calls?

HARMONY

Just a few. But it's *so* obvious. You don't change anything in your life. You've eaten the same meals all month. You always skip dessert. I bet you wait three dates before having sex.

CHARLIE gasps.

CHARLIE

Well...I...that...so what if I did? It's all none of your business!

HARMONY

Just trying to help.

CHARLIE

Well you're not! I'm expecting my fiancée to Facetime any minute. Could you please leave?

HARMONY

(shrugs shoulders and heads to her room) I'll create a change spell for you. You'll love it. You'll see.

CHARLIE flops back down on the sofa, pours herself more wine, and downs most of the glass. One of her cats hops up and makes himself comfortable on her oversized white skirt, and she lovingly pats him, gives him a kiss, not worrying about the dress. The tablet rings and she answers, bringing up STERLING's face on the screen. He's mid 40s, smart looking, in a jacket and tie at a corporate desk, a dark sky through the large window behind him.

CHARLIE

Sweetie? Why aren't you here yet?

STERLING

I got tied up. It couldn't be helped.

CHARLIE

You always say that. Will you say

that on our wedding day?

She puts her hands to her chest and looks down
at herself, realizing she's in her dress.

CHARLIE (CONT'D)

Oh shit!

She covers herself with a red throw. STERLING
is looking down at a stack of reports, not even
cluing in that she's in her future wedding gown.

STERLING

Hmm? What's that? Are you still upset? I said it
couldn't be helped. Look, I'll buy you dinner
and flowers tomorrow night. They'll be cheaper
then anyway.

He chuckles awkwardly and returns to his
reports. CHARLIE holds up a DVD romance

they were going to watch and the box of half-eaten chocolates.

STERLING (CONT'D)

Darling. It's just another day created by greeting card companies. We don't have to buy into the bullshit.

CHARLIE picks up the tablet, stands, hoists the top of her dress with one hand, glares into STERLING's shocked eyes as she starts to shout.

CHARLIE

But I want to buy into it! I know it's bullshit, okay? But it's bullshit that feeds my tired, cynical soul! The man I spent a decade of my life with is dead. Dead! From a collision with a driver who was high out of his mind! So maybe I need the romantic bullshit to dull the pain.

CHARLIE starts to quietly cry. But she doesn't like crying, so she decides to be angry instead.

CHARLIE (CONT'D)

Give me that romantic bullshit over sitting here alone night after night eating Oreo ice cream in fleece pajamas, reading Instagram posts about how Kate Middleton's skin is glowing and dewy and not too matte! AND another thing. I HATE IT WHEN YOU CALL ME DARLING!

STERLING has already hung up on his end of the call, halfway through CHARLIE's tirade. CHARLIE stares at the black screen.

CHARLIE

There it is. You're always leaving.

HARMONY appears in her doorway. She's still wearing black lipstick and a night shirt that reads SATAN IS MY SUGAR DADDY.

HARMONY

Did I hear you say we've got ice cream?

CHARLIE shakes her head, exasperated, closes the tablet, flops down on the sofa and picks up her phone. She's made a life-changing decision. She picks up the stuffed penguin and drunkenly tells him:

CHARLIE

That's it. I'm texting him back.

INT. YOGA STUDIO, NEW YORK - DAY

CHARLIE enters the lobby of a busy yoga studio. Two YOGA INSTRUCTORS are behind the front counter registering people for the next class. SHARON and JUSTINE are sitting on yoga cushions sipping ginger tea. SHARON's dabbing her eyes with a tissue. Her eyes are red from crying, and JUSTINE's are not much better. CHARLIE hangs up her hat and jacket, tosses her bag aside and sits beside SHARON. She starts to rub her back.

CHARLIE

Woah. Class brought out that much emotion, huh?

SHARON

No, pilates with Justine was great.

She's such a patient teacher.

JUSTINE smiles faintly and bows her head, acknowledging the compliment.

SHARON (CONT'D)

You doing yoga flow before your shift at the hotel?

CHARLIE

I was going to, but you look like you need me to be here more.

SHARON

I'll be fine!

JUSTINE

She's not fine.

SHARON

Well neither are you!

CHARLIE laughs and pours herself some tea.

CHARLIE

That makes three of us. What did he do this time?

SHARON looks around making sure no one else is coming to sit with them. Everyone else in the lobby is occupied. She still lowers her voice.

SHARON

Sly prat tried to sell the house, right from under me!

CHARLIE

What?

SHARON

Internet gambling. He's used the entire line of credit, and he's another 70 K in debt.

CHARLIE

Sweetie, oh my God that's horrible.

JUSTINE looks her friend up and down. She's known her so long, she can read her.

JUSTINE

You seem off. You're having reservations about your wedding.

CHARLIE nods, glancing at the phone in her hand.

CHARLIE

I thought I loved STERLING, but maybe I'm in love with the idea of love more. I got swept up in the idea of this wedding. Oh. I'm awful! I'm a wedding-loving whore.

JUSTINE

Honey, that's so not true. I've known you all my life, and I've only witnessed you being a whore.

This gets the ladies laughing for the first time in hours.

CHARLIE

(still laughing) Are you two slut shaming me?

SHARON

Hell no, we applaud it! But we may have to cancel you for your fashion fails.

CHARLIE

Those leather pants in '04 were a definite low point.

JUSTINE

Didn't you flash your ass to the DJ

by accident?

CHARLIE

Who says it was by accident?

SHARON

Okay, okay, back to our harsh reality. Don't marry him Charlie! We all know he's not right for you. Just move somewhere cheaper. Move in with me! We have to sell. I need a new place.

JUSTINE

Me too. Jerry's been cheating for months. He sent me a text asking for an open marriage, but I got it six months late.

CHARLIE and SHARON are taken aback. SHARON puts her tea down and stares at her friend.

SHARON

Wait, what? Allan says the text I got from him yesterday was sent six months ago, too!

YOGA INSTRUCTOR 1 is passing by and overhears the conversation.

YOGA INSTRUCTOR 1

Isn't it wild? 170,000 texts were in queue for six months. Six months! Now everyone's love life's in downward facing dog.

CHARLIE

What are you talking about?

YOGA INSTRUCTOR 2 clicks a remote and turns on the flat wall TV near where the group has gathered.

YOGA INSTRUCTOR 2

It should be on the news. It's the top story on every channel today.

Everyone turns to watch.

NEWSCAST WOMAN

If you woke up on Valentine's Day to a weird text that seemed totally out of place, you aren't alone. A mysterious wave of messages, 170,000 in total, swept America's phones overnight, delivering confusing, mixed messages from friends, family and the occasional ex.

INT. NEW YORK CAFÉ - DAY

CUT TO:

Two women are at a small table in a café with Valentines- hearts hanging from the window. They are scrolling their phones while holding hands, but when one shows the other her phone, she pulls her hand away. They start arguing. Other couples of a range of ages and ethnicities are scrolling their phones in the café, suddenly finding themselves in heated discussions as well.

NEWSCAST WOMAN (V.O.)

Friends who hadn't talked to each other in months were jolted into chatting. Others briefly panicked as their ex-Valentines contacted them once again. The messages were all sent on

August 14th. Spokespeople for two major carriers said the six-month delay resulted from a "maintenance update" and would not explain further, calling it a "third-party vendor issue."

INT. YOGA STUDIO, NEW YORK - DAY

CHARLIE

What the William Shatner!

BACK TO:

CUT TO:

SHARON

What happened to you using Barbara Streisand to swear?

JUSTINE

Yeah I thought Streisand was catchier...

CHARLIE

(stands, tapping her phone to unlock it, panicked) Fuck Barbara Streisand! I'm completely fucked!

JUSTINE stands, walks over to her friend, pries the phone from her hand and talks her down.

JUSTINE

Whatever you want to text, don't do it. You'll regret it.

CHARLIE starts pacing.

CHARLIE

I already do, that's the problem! I texted back my high school boyfriend on Valentine's Day and said I wanted to meet him. Actually, I might have texted a little more than that. I was piss drunk. And angry at Sterling.

SHARON quietly sips her tea, looking up at her two friends.

SHARON

You want to leave your rich fiancée to meet a

man you loved 20 years ago. I'd say you win the Mid-Life Crisis Challenge. Essential oil?

SHARON takes a small bottle of peppermint oil and sniffs it, offers it to CHARLIE then puts it down when she sees CHARLIE isn't laughing. She stands up and wraps her arms around her.

SHARON (CONT'D)

Aw come on you know I'm kidding, I'm just as pathetic. I'd move back to the UK and live with me Mum and two grown daughters if it weren't for you maniacal muggles.

JUSTINE is scanning her friend's messages. She's done this before.

JUSTINE

So, who is it? Is it Doug? The one who always called you Chubby Charlie? Because if it's Doug, I bet he's fat, balding, and sells used cars.

CHARLIE shakes her head. JUSTINE is looking down at the screen. She's reading CHARLIE's texts and laughing. Hard.

JUSTINE (CONT'D)

It's not Doug. It's Dayton Hill! And you wrote him that you'd, and I quote, "seen the jogging photos and they very nearly made me cream my panties."

CHARLIE covers her mouth in horror.

CHARLIE

I wrote what?

SHARON tries to spit her ginger tea back into the small cup without success. She's choking and laughing at once. JUSTINE stifles giggles and reads the text out loud.

JUSTINE

You wrote that his ass was, "a hot mound of molten lava in spandex"

Sharon gasps.

SHARON

THE Dayton Hill? The rock star Dayton Hill? You went to high school with him?

JUSTINE

I think you should be more concerned that she drunk-texted him and inferred he's got a lumpy ass.

CHARLIE grabs her phone back and starts pacing again.

CHARLIE

We dated the summer after graduation. Last summer he shows up at our reunion. Came in the back entrance.

SHARON

And you gave him your number?

CHARLIE

Well, we slow danced, and...

SHARON

You danced?

CHARLIE

I couldn't not. I was swept off my feet. He's written 15 albums with the same band and people still love him as much as they did on his first. He's changed the music industry!

JUSTINE

Rolling Stone magazine once wrote that he WAS the music industry.

CHARLIE

See? How could I say no to his beautiful face? Besides, I wasn't with Sterling yet. And I didn't give the number. It was on all the printed reunion info. I was a coordinator.

SHARON

I knew he was from around here, but didn't know you went to school with him. I pay more attention to my UK stars back home. Love me my Royals.

JUSTINE

I missed the reunion, but I was checking out our yearbook over Christmas. It's like he hasn't aged since his first album 20 years ago. He's smart and single and in one word...

JUSTINE opens her own phone, does a fast search and shows SHARON the jogging photo in question. Dayton Hill, 40, is shirtless, tanned, toned and tattooed, running alongside a lake.

SHARON AND JUSTINE IN UNISON
Breathtaking.

CHARLIE sighs and falls backwards to the couch. She's miserable.

CHARLIE
And I sexted him last night, six months too late.

JUSTINE

Girl, you're so fucked.

SHARON

And I thought we'd had bad luck.

They're still chuckling, but JUSTINE is rubbing CHARLIE's back in loving empathy.

JUSTINE

We have to leave our men and find somewhere to stay. Meanwhile, you've burst open a volcano of hot molten lava.

CHARLIE groans, slithers back into the sofa and covers her face with a pillow. JUSTINE looks solemn. She glances at her phone, then back up to her friends. SHARON and JUSTINE sit back down, slumping into the sofa.

JUSTINE (CONT'D)

It's my fucking fortieth birthday tomorrow night

AND it's Valentine's weekend, and I don't know who I am or where I live anymore.

SHARON

What? You're the first of us to turn forty?

CHARLIE

I knew that. I knew that! I booked a suite for us at the Bellevue. It was gonna be a surprise. I get an employee discount. The guys were going to join us but...

JUSTINE sits up straighter.

JUSTINE

Screw them!

SHARON

I second that. You should celebrate birthdays with the people who truly see you.

As JUSTINE stands, CHARLIE joins her, wrapping an arm around her.

CHARLIE

I see you, you beautiful Goddesses! And I see that I need to get away from my witchy roommate! Let's get the party started early.

SHARON swipes a few essential oil bottles off the table, puts them in her bag, buttons her jacket and stands with newfound energy, ready to leave, ready to start a new life.

SHARON

Just how early is early check in, and can we hit the wine store on the way?

INT. NEW YORK BELLEVUE BANQUET HALL - EVENING

A large and airy luxury hotel banquet hall. CHARLIE is in a black skirt and white dress shirt with the hotel logo on the chest, her hair up in a neat bun. She's arranging red and pink roses in delicate pitchers beside small glass lanterns on the tables. The tables are covered in crisp white tablecloths and the chairs have white covers with bows on the back. The hotel manager MITCH, 50, tall, good-looking, white haired, Welsh accent though he's lived in the US twenty years, comes bustling into the room.

MITCH

How's it going in here? Looks great.

CHARLIE

The cake got made in time, and it's beautiful.

MITCH looks at a gorgeous three-layer Valentine's themed cake on a table in the corner and smiles with satisfaction.

CHARLIE (CONT'D)

Just waiting for the band now. I think Lucas, the groom, will be pleased with everything.

MITCH

And the bride?

CHARLIE

I'm hiding upstairs unless there's an emergency.
I think she coined the term Bridezilla. It might
be her maiden name.

MITCH laughs and shakes her hand.

MITCH

Thanks for the great work Charlie. Keep this up
and you'll be our full- time wedding
coordinator. For the whole chain.

CHARLIE

Wow, that'd be great. I could really use the
money.

MITCH

Keep impressing me and it's a real possibility.
So, Don at front desk says you've booked a
Presidential suite?

CHARLIE

Yeah...for me and two friends. The discount rate

helps, thanks. We're going apartment shopping tomorrow.

MITCH

No problem. I didn't think a suite would be available February 15th, but now the entire wedding party is flying out to Vegas after the reception, so the whole floor's open. I'll hold the room and see if we can discount it further for you. You deserve it. You're a stellar employee.

CHARLIE smiles, then glances down at her phone on the table. A call is coming in on silent mode, and it's from STERLING. She presses decline.

CHARLIE

I uh...I.have to un-book this reception room for August. I'm so sorry for the change.

MITCH

Oh. Oh Charlie. I'm sorry. What happened?

CHARLIE

I woke up.

MITCH

That's a good thing to happen before you walk down the aisle, but I'm still sorry.

CHARLIE

Me too, Mitch, me too.

MITCH walks toward the double doors. CHARLIE straightens a fork and knife on the table in front of her.

MITCH

Charlie?

CHARLIE

Yeah boss?

MITCH

It wasn't my place to say anything before, but I always thought Sterling was a stuck-up prat. You deserve better. He made my chef remake his salad three times. Three times! Because the ratio of cheese to dressing wasn't right. Who does that?

Charlie laughs.

CHARLIE

I know. You should have heard him go on about the toilet paper rolls in my place hanging wrong.

MITCH rolls his eyes.

MITCH

What did he want, origami?

He gives her a wink, and leaves the room.

CHARLIE's phone buzzes on the table. She glares at it like it's a person, not wanting to answer it again. STERLING enters the double doors in a flurry of ego. He's holding a dozen red roses.

STERLING

Pookeypoo, why are you not answering my calls?

CHARLIE turns around. She didn't want to have to do this here.

CHARLIE

I don't think we...Sterling, I can't marry you.

STERLING

What the fuck are you talking about?

STERLING slams the roses on a table. Petals fall to the floor.

CHARLIE motions for him to come over to a corner of the banquet hall. He folds his arms and refuses.

CHARLIE

We aren't compatible. You work all the time and when you're not working, you're talking about working. I lost one husband already. I don't want to lose you too!

STERLING

So don't. We'll move in together. Cancel the wedding, and we'll live together. Then you'll see me more.

CHARLIE's face falls.

CHARLIE

I don't want to see you anymore. I need something different.

STERLING

Or someone different! Who are you seeing?

CHARLIE

No one! Sterling, can we not argue about this at my work?

STERLING

Fine. It's over. Don't come running back to me when your life's in shambles.

CHARLIE takes off her engagement ring and gives it back. He storms off, but turns to speak at the doors before leaving.

STERLING (CONT'D)

I was about to take you out for an expensive dinner. Like you're always nagging me about!

CHARLIE

Well, you won't have to listen to the old hag anymore!

CHARLIE's crying but trying to hold back the tears. She wipes her face with the back of a hand, wipes her hand on her skirt, tries to compose herself, and gets back to anxiously rearranging the table flowers and lantern, putting them in a different place and then the exact place they had already been.

CHARLIE (CONT'D)

(Muttering to herself) Resistant to change, my ass. I am SO not resistant to change anymore.

BRIDEZILLA and her groom LUCAS burst into the room. She giggles as her groom tries to kiss her neck. He's not succeeding in getting very close to her because she is in the most elaborate poofy wedding gown you can imagine.

BRIDEZILLA

Hey chic-a! We sealed the deal!

She holds up her hand, displaying her new wedding band. LUCAS kisses it.

CHARLIE sniffles, then speaks.

CHARLIE

Congrats! The hall's all yours. I'll be in a suite upstairs, just call if you need anything.

Just then CHARLIE's phone buzzes again. She picks it up fast.

CHARLIE (CONT'D)

Sterling you can't keep calling me at work like...oh, hello! What? No, no, please, you can't, the reception's in an hour and a half.

BRIDEZILLA's eyes nearly pop out of their sockets. She shoves her affectionate husband aside to hear what CHARLIE is saying.

CHARLIE (CONT'D)

Yes, I understand. No one can sing with laryngitis. Feel better.

CHARLIE puts the phone down and looks at BRIDEZILLA. BRIDEZILLA is livid.

CHARLIE bites her lower lip, trying to find the words.

LUCAS

Sweetheart, I could sing if...

BRIDEZILLA

Your singing makes my ears bleed. Just shut up.

CHARLIE

Guys, I can fix this. Give me half an hour. I can fix this.

CHARLIE looks calm. She's skilled at hiding her panicked state. She gently guides the couple out the doors to the lobby where she spots MITCH.

INT. HOTEL LOBBY - EVENING

CHARLIE

MITCH, we've hit a slight snag with the wedding singer. These two need their coats, a drink, and to meet their photographer in the garden.

MITCH

I'll get them champagne and take them there. I won't even ask. You've got this.

MITCH is at the closet behind the desk, pulling the bride's hooded white fur cloak off a hanger.

CHARLIE

Please don't ask. But yes, I've got this.

BRIDEZILLA grabs the cloak from MITCH's hands.

BRIDEZILLA

You'd better! Or I'll see that you never work again.

CHARLIE gets on the elevator. The second the doors close, she leans against the mirrored back wall and starts speaking to herself.

CHARLIE

I've got this? I've got this? The fuck I've got
this!

INT. PRESIDENTIAL SUITE - EVENING

CHARLIE bangs on the door. SHARON,
wearing a luxurious white hotel robe,
champagne in hand, opens it. CHARLIE rushes
in.

CHARLIE

I left STERLING.

SHARON

Good decision. Long overdue!

CHARLIE

And the wedding singer's sick.

SHARON

But isn't the reception...

CHARLIE

Yes. All the fucking people are on their fucking way!

CHARLIE flops on the sectional couch and puts her head in her hands. JUSTINE, cosmopolitan in hand, sits calmly beside her.

JUSTINE

Well, he may be older than the dude you booked, but he *has* been called a legend.

CHARLIE

Who are you talking about?

JUSTINE

Your ex? The one you just recently got in touch with?

CHARLIE

Dayton! Oh no. No no no. I can't ask him to fill in!

SHARON, already tipsy, giggles and puts a
loving arm around her friend.

SHARON

Sure you can. You told him he had a volcanic
ass. You could ask him to play Carnegie Hall on
the moon, if you want!

SHARON and JUSTINE start laughing, until
JUSTINE's face falls. She gets serious.

JUSTINE

I just got off the phone with Jerry and we're
divorcing.

SHARON

Oh, doll. So sorry. It's over for us too. Allan
finally agreed to see a counselor for his
addiction.

JUSTINE

(sad realization) Suddenly, we're all single.

CHARLIE

If I'm honest about it, I've been alone for a long time now.

SHARON

Same. I'll always be his friend, but I won't enable him anymore.

JUSTINE

What we need is a pick-me-up. A party with a rock star! And selfishly...it would make my birthday unforgettable! What are you waiting for?

SHARON keeps giggling. CHARLIE looks at her phone in her hand, then looks at each of her friends for a moment. They fall silent in anticipation as she mulls it over. Mind made up, she stands.

CHARLIE

I'm doing this. It's crazy, but it's worth a shot.

JUSTINE

You go girl!

SHARON

You won't regret it!

CHARLIE is standing at the bathroom door. She answers Sharon, speaking as she closes it shut.

CHARLIE

Oh, I bet I will. But if this works, we're gonna have the birthday bash of our dreams.

INT. PRESIDENTIAL SUITE BATHROOM - EVENING

CHARLIE paces the large hotel bathroom for a moment before sitting on the toilet, taking a dramatic deep breath, head between knees, lifting her head, exhaling, and dialing DAYTON's number.

CHARLIE

(Taking one more deep breath) I am

open to change. I am open to change!

CHARLIE (CONT'D)

(Hearing him answer) Dayton? It's Charlie. I

know you just got the strangest text from me...

INT. GREENWICH VILLAGE, NY -
PENTHOUSE - EVENING

DAYTON HILL, an attractive 40-year old man

in fitted jeans and white t-shirt, elegant Celtic

tattoos on his neck and arms, is on his cell

phone looking out his wall to ceiling windows.

DAYTON

It was strange and sensual and beautiful.

Charlie...could we vid instead?

DAYTON presses the video camera request.

INT. PRESIDENTIAL SUITE BATHROOM - EVENING

CHARLIE (laughs)

I'm sitting on the toilet! I mean not really! I'm sitting here freaking out...

DAYTON

Please. I need to see you again...

CHARLIE takes a deep breath, then accepts the video request.

CHARLIE

(Looks at DAYTON on her phone) Hi.

DAYTON

Hi there. What I wanted to say to your face was...I wish you hadn't waited six months to reply...(hesitates) but more than anything, I wish my damned obsession with something as fleeting as success hadn't taken me away from you all these years...

CHARLIE

Your text came late! Like six months late! I wasn't supposed to read it now!

DAYTON

(laughs) I wasn't aware texts had Best Before dates.

CHARLIE

Considering thousands of people are being thrown off course today, I think it should be a law! I'll explain later.

DAYTON

So we can meet up later?

CHARLIE

Actually, would now work for you? Like, right now?

DAYTON

Band's on a break. I'm free as a bird. Actually...

He hesitates, runs a hand through his hair. Then he thinks better of what we was going to say and stops speaking.

CHARLIE

I'll never ask you this kind of colossal favor again, but the entertainment just cancelled on the big Bellevue wedding reception I coordinated, and the show starts in an hour...

DAYTON

I'm already there, Whirl-a-girl.

CHARLIE

Dayton, I'm not that same girl...Twenty

years changes a woman. I'm starting to go grey. Everything's sagging. And...

DAYTON

And what does any of this have to do with me still loving you, and you wanting to spank me in my spandex?

CHARLIE chuckles and smiles for the first time in hours. It's a wide smile, full of relief. She feels seen. She's tearing up.

CHARLIE

Nothing. You're right, none of that matters.

DAYTON

Oh, shit. I forgot my driver's headed to the airport. Took the weekend off. Besides, a limo in the Village makes too much of a scene. Can you pick me up?

CHARLIE

You want me to be your driver? Do you not remember what you thought about my driving?

DAYTON

I remember how you made me feel. I don't recall how you handled a stick shift.

CHARLIE

If that's a dirty joke we don't have time for
those.

She pauses, looking concerned.

CHARLIE (CONT'D)

And there's something else you should know...

DAYTON

Whatever it is we can deal with it. I'll call Sean,
see if he's up to playing a gig tonight. Can you
make it to the Village in time?

CHARLIE glances at the digital clock in the
mirror and inhales deeply.

CHARLIE

First time for everything. Get your lavalicious
ass ready, rock star. My job depends on it.

DAYTON

I'll text the address. I'll be waiting inside the
doors.

INT. CHARLIE'S APARTMENT - EVENING

CHARLIE races into the apartment, car keys in hand, and scurries to her room. She grabs a suitcase and shoves a black dress, jeans, tops, panties, socks, toothpaste and toiletries inside. HARMONY arrives in her doorway, phone in one hand, burning sage smudge stick in the other.

HARMONY

Taking a trip?

CHARLIE

Not that it's your business, but, no. I'm staying over at the Bellevue. My big wedding needs some help.

HARMONY

I could help. I can cleanse the room.

CHARLIE

No no, it's fully cleansed, thanks Harmony.

HARMONY

Wait. What's the date?

CHARLIE

It's the fifteenth, and I really don't have time for this! Please feed the cats for me. I'll take money off your rent.

HARMONY

You're in charge of tonight's wedding at the Bellevue Banquet Hall?

CHARLIE

Not if I don't get there in the next forty minutes!

CHARLIE rushes out the door. HARMONY leans against the back of the door, re-reading a thread of messages on her phone:

LUCAS

<Harm! I miss you baby! Let's get back together!>

HARMONY

<Still love you too! Wasn't expecting this>

LUCAS

<WTH? Me neither! Getting married

Feb. 15th. Huge Bellevue wedding. Duck! Stop texting me.

HARMONY puts her phone to sleep and makes a heart shape with the smudge stick smoke. She frowns.

HARMONY

Bippity, Boppity, Boo.

She blows on the smoke, destroying the heart shape.

INT. CHARLIE'S USED VOLKSWAGON BEETLE - EVENING

CHARLIE is in her used, hot-pink painted Volkswagon beetle. It's old and rusty in places, but well-loved and decorated with eyelashes on the headlights. She sees DAYTON inside the glassed-in lobby at her destination on the right and tries to parallel park slowly. She hits the curb hard with her right wheel. Flustered, she turns off the car.

CHARLIE

BARBARA FUCKING STREISAND!

EXT. GREENWICH VILLAGE STREET - EVENING

DAYTON, dressed in jeans, a white shirt, a baseball cap and shades, is shaking his head and chuckling. He can hear CHARLIE swearing as he strolls up to the car, since her window's rolled open.

CHARLIE is trying to turn the car back on, but it's choking. She talks to her car like she's an old friend.

CHARLIE

Come on, come on, don't let me down old girl.

DAYTON breaks into deeper laughter as he studies the car more fully, then opens the passenger door. The car finally starts, still sputtering a little. CHARLIE's hiding her face in her hands as he settles in.

DAYTON

I can't decide who's more adorable:

you or your car.

CHARLIE

Get in! There could be Paparazzi.

He's barely inside when CHARLIE pulls off the curb and speeds away.

INT. CHARLIE'S USED VOLKSWAGEN BEETLE - EVENING Dayton adjusts his sunglasses nervously.

DAYTON

If you don't want the paparazzi trailing us, it would be wise not to hit any little old ladies...

CHARLIE

Just the ones that get in my way.

DAYTON laughs, makes sure his belt is on, slinks down in his seat.

DAYTON

Still fearless, I see.

CHARLIE grins at him.

CHARLIE

Don't puke in Priscilla.

DAYTON can't take his eyes off CHARLIE. He chuckles.

DAYTON

You named your car Priscilla?

CHARLIE

Presley. What? She's a strong woman. Like this car. Been through a lot. I admire her greatly.

She swerves suddenly.

DAYTON

I'd like to say I admire you, too, but I'm trying to keep down the Cornish Yarg I ate earlier.

She laughs and looks at him, then pulls his cap lower over his head for him, and screeches through a yellow light.

CHARLIE

You eat the strangest things!

DAYTON

You drive like a headless monkey!

CHARLIE

Some things never change. Hold onto

your horses, bucko!

EXT. BELLEVUE HOTEL ENTRANCE -
EVENING

Priscilla the pink car with CHARLIE driving
zooms into a parallel park in front of the hotel
and the right front tire bumps the curb again.

CHARLIE is swearing at herself inside the car.
DAYTON and SEAN, who is now in the back
seat holding a guitar case, are laughing
hysterically.

CHARLIE, DAYTON and SEAN rush out of
the car, slamming the doors. DAYTON goes to
the trunk and grabs CHARLIE's suitcase for
her. He and SEAN carry their guitars in cases on
their backs and are wearing baseball caps and

shades, hunched over as they run to the front doors, which a DOORMAN opens for them.

A CUTE OLD MAN VALET takes the keys from CHARLIE, and at that very moment, an eyelash falls off of one of Priscilla's headlights. CHARLIE looks over her shoulder as she runs into the hotel.

CHARLIE

Sorry Priscilla, I promise I'll take you to the salon later!

The CUTE OLD MAN VALET looks perplexed as to why everyone is racing into the hotel. He checks out the car as if it were a woman and slowly picks up the eyelash off the pavement. He taps the top of the car and gets inside, eyelash in hand, and strokes the steering wheel.

OLD VALET

About to kick the bucket too, huh? (whispers)

Even without the eyelash, I'd take you to the dance.

He turns on the ignition and she turns on easily and sounds like she's purring on the first try. CUTE OLD MAN VALET looks pleased with himself.

INT. BELLEVUE HOTEL BANQUET HALL - EVENING

BRIDEZILLA and LUCAS are sitting at the wedding party table, flanked by best men and bridesmaids on each side. BRIDEZILLA is all smiles and waves to her friends in the crowd; LUCAS looks slightly miserable, keeps glancing at his phone.

They are eating the main course. There's a jovial murmur in the crowd of about 150. No one knows anything is wrong.

CHARLIE, who has changed into a knee-length black spaghetti strapped dress, discreetly enters the hall and comes up behind the couple. She bends to whisper to them.

CHARLIE

I've fixed the issue. Dayton Hill will be singing for you in a few minutes.

BRIDEZILLA stands up, squeals and turns to look at the blue- curtained-off stage in the far corner.

BRIDEZILLA

(loudly)THE DAYTON HILL? Are you kidding me?

CHARLIE

(lowers her voice) I was going to announce him, but that'll do fine.

BRIDEZILLA claps and jumps up and down. The guests all stand in anticipation. LUCAS stays seated, staring at his phone. He's not enjoying himself. BRIDEZILLA smacks him on his upper arm.

BRIDEZILLA

Lucas, stand up, it's Dayton Hill!

BRIDEZILLA turns to CHARLIE, squeals again and gives her a tight hug. CHARLIE's expression over BRIDEZILLA's shoulder looks uncomfortable and nervous.

CHARLIE

They haven't done a sound check or

anything. I just hope it's good...

BRIDEZILLA

They?

CHARLIE

Yeah, Sean made it here too. He's going to be on acoustic.

BRIDEZILLA

Dayton AND Sean. Omeeegod! My wedding is EPIC!

CHARLIE

Just remember it was last minute...

An acoustic guitar starts to play a slow, seductive intro. We hear the first few chords of an electric guitar accompanying the first guitar. The blue curtain starts opening.

SHARON and JUSTINE come running into the banquet hall. They're in little black dresses and heels. They pull CHARLIE to the stage area, giggling, and remain close, elbows locked. They're full of giddy anticipation.

The curtain opens fully, and DAYTON appears playing a white electric guitar, gorgeous in a black sports jacket, black shirt and tie, sexy tattoos visible on his neck, beaming at the crowd. SEAN is in a white shirt and jeans,

playing the acoustic beside him. DAYTON
winks at CHARLIE first, then looks to the bride
and LUCAS and nods at them.

DAYTON

Congratulations to the happy

couple. You might know this one. Let's get this
party started!

DAYTON starts to sing his greatest hit, a
Maroon 5 style rock song. The crowd goes wild.
People get up quickly and soon the dance floor
is full. His voice is incredible and the song
uplifting, memorable.

MITCH comes into the hall and stands there
taking in the scene, hands on hips, laughing,
very pleased. He notices SHARON dancing on
her own and we see a spark in his eye.

JUSTINE starts laughing and crying simultaneously and throws her arms around CHARLIE.

CHARLIE

Happy birthday, beautiful!

With BRIDEZILLA motioning them to join her, most of the partygoers get into a line formation, hands on one another's hips, and make their way around the room, laughing and kicking their feet left and right as the song plays out in full.

When the song ends, SEAN starts playing an intricate acoustic solo and the crowd stops and watches, mesmerized. With everyone's attention on SEAN's beautiful solo, CHARLIE discreetly pulls DAYTON into a tiny galley kitchen off the banquet hall.

INT. BELLEVUE HOTEL BANQUET HALL KITCHEN - NIGHT

The modern galley kitchen is dimly lit. CHARLIE faces DAYTON, pulling his hands in hers, up close to her face.

CHARLIE

Your hands are shaking! Were you nervous?

DAYTON lets go of CHARLIE's hands, leans his back against the counter and offers her a chocolate covered strawberry off a platter.

DAYTON

Sure was. Most days I wake up feeling old and obsolete.

CHARLIE

(Hesitating to take the strawberry)

Oh yeah, I never eat dessert...Wait. You know what? What the hell!

DAYTON

Good decision.

CHARLIE takes the strawberry and they both eat one, smiling with their eyes at how sweet they are. They're sharing a delicious moment.

CHARLIE

(Wipes her mouth) I wake up like that too. But didn't you hear them? They loved you!

DAYTON

(Chuckles) Yeah. That'll keep me going at least another year.

CHARLIE

I guess it's like anything in life. You just have to savor the good times while you can.

DAYTON

(Putting a new strawberry to

CHARLIE's lips) Savor them, like a chocolate covered strawberry?

CHARLIE

(closes her eyes and lets him feed her the berry)

Mmmmm. Like that. I forgot how much I love dessert!

DAYTON laughs with her.

DAYTON

Charlie. I was nervous for another

reason.

He pulls her closer and looks down at her. He's turned serious.

DAYTON (CONT'D)

In that drunken mess of a text, you mentioned you're moving in with your boyfriend...

CHARLIE looks up into his eyes, smiling.

CHARLIE

Not anymore. My current address is right here. With you.

DAYTON

I like the sound of that.

DAYTON cups her chin and kisses her. It's like their first kiss 20 years ago, but even more passionate, and it lasts longer.

DAYTON (CONT'D)

And now I'm calm.

CHARLIE

And now I feel nineteen again.

They kiss again. Dayton's hands slide from her hair, down the sides of her dress, resting on her bchind.

DAYTON

(reluctantly) I should go.

He keeps kissing her. They both can't stop. CHARLIE finally pulls away.

CHARLIE (CONT'D)

Go give them what they want, so I can have you all to myself later.

INT. BELLEVUE HOTEL LOBBY - NIGHT

Guitars play in the background: DAYTON is beginning a new rock song accompanied by SEAN in the banquet hall. The crowd cheers.

The HOTEL FRONT DESK CLERK nods as HARMONY enters through the front glass doors, dressed in one of CHARLIE's white shirts with the hotel logo on the chest and a black skirt. She smiles sweetly at him.

HARMONY

I'm supposed to be working tonight's wedding to help Charlie out. She needed extra help.

HOTEL FRONT DESK CLERK

Well supper's been served but I guess you can help at the bar...

FRONT DESK CLERK leaves the desk and motions for her to follow him to the correct banquet hall.

HARMONY

Yeah, sure. I'm good with all the mixing.

HOTEL FRONT DESK CLERK looks at her oddly but opens the banquet hall door and they walk inside. As they do, a REPORTER with a camera strapped around his neck rushes through the unattended lobby and slips in right behind them, sliding into a dark corner.

INT. BELLEVUE HOTEL BANQUET HALL - NIGHT

DAYTON finishes the last rock song and people on the dance floor stop and applaud him, including BRIDEZILLA and LUCAS.

LUCAS gets a panicked look on his face. He drops BRIDEZILLA's hand and mouths GO! to

HARMONY who's hiding in the darkest corner of the hall, pulling sage and sweetgrass smudge sticks out of her backpack. When she doesn't budge, he discreetly leaves the dance floor. BRIDEZILLA has her eyes on DAYTON as the applause simmers.

DAYTON

Thank you. This has been a night we won't forget!

He pauses for a moment, looking down at his feet. He's unsure of his next song. We see him gathering courage.

DAYTON (CONT'D)

Speaking of things you don't forget, this song is for someone I lost sight of for a while, but never forgot.

DAYTON turns to SEAN and whispers:

DAYTON (CONT'D)

It's the one I was working on last week, just follow my lead.

SEAN

Can-do, bro.

DAYTON starts to sing a beautiful rock love ballad. It's about realizing how much someone has meant to you all your life. The sound is reminiscent of Bon Jovi's "Always" or Aerosmith "Don't Wanna Miss A Thing."

DAYTON

(singing)If I could turn back time, I'd spend my life with you. Like sea reaching for the sand, there's nothing I wouldn't do.

The song is dreamy, mesmerizing.

Charlie inhales and exhales deeply; as she watches him she realizes that something in her life has changed this very second.

MITCH is also on the dance floor, twirling and dipping SHARON to the melody. He is a big dork and she adores it. After he dips her they laugh and she caresses his chest in a flirty manner. MITCH notices she's thirsty and pours her a tall glass of water from a pitcher on a nearby table.

SHARON

You spoil me!

MITCH

You deserve it. All of it.

SHARON drinks the water, eyes lustily locked on him, puts out her hand and MITCH kisses it, then spins her around the dance floor again. They're having the time of their lives.

SHARON

This is going to sound strange, but, do you have any addictions?

MITCH

Nope. You're going to be my first.

SHARON

(laughs joyfully) Oh go on!

MITCH pulls her in close to him and they gaze adoringly into each other's eyes.

JUSTINE is standing in a dark corner deep in conversation with a hot younger man, TROY in his early 30s. He is charming and totally into her. He is showing her his phone with a NEW SCIENTIST article on it, instead of being into his phone all himself.

TROY

So you think that it's possible?

JUSTINE

Why not? Perseverance rover runs on processors from 1990s iMacs.

TROY

Smart and beautiful. Stroke of luck that my plus-one cancelled tonight.

JUSTINE

(smirking) Did she cancel by text?

TROY

No, I hardly ever text. I like my conversations in- person, why?

JUSTINE (CONT'D)

Just checking.

She grabs his face and kisses him. He's not complaining at all.

The song ends to fervent applause, and DAYTON hands SEAN his guitar and mutters something to him. SEAN nods and gives him a wink. SEAN breaks into a riveting electric guitar solo that has everyone's attention except that of LUCAS and HARMONY, who are in heated discussion in the dark corner.

DAYTON slips off the stage, takes CHARLIE's hand and they leave the hall, giggling and all over each other like newlyweds.

INT. PRESIDENTIAL SUITE BATHROOM - NIGHT

We can hear and see the large glass shower running, creating steam in the room. CHARLIE has her back against the marble- top bathroom counter. DAYTON is shirtless and on his knees, head against her belly.

DAYTON slowly rolls her dress up and over her head as he also rises, giving her kisses from her bellybutton up to her bare breasts as he does so. When he reaches her neck, she arches back in ecstasy and he slowly kisses it, then her lips.

The room is getting foggy and as CHARLIE and DAYTON make love on the counter, CHARLIES's hands make streak prints down the foggy mirror and the scene fades out.

INT. PRESIDENTIAL SUITE BEDROOM - NIGHT

CHARLIE is naked on the King bed under a white sheet, lying on her side facing DAYTON, also on his side. Their eyes are locked.

CHARLIE

I don't usually do that on the first date.

DAYTON

(chuckles) I love that you broke the rules for me. But I'm not sure what we just did there could be considered *dating*. I think we skipped a few steps.

CHARLIE

And a few years...My God! All these years. What made you come back for me?

DAYTON

Oh, my love. I never truly left.

CHARLIE

It sure felt like it...

DAYTON

It was my career that took me away from you. And I'm so sorry about that.

CHARLIE

You don't have to apologize. Life is full of rotten luck.

DAYTON

(props himself up higher on his

pillow) I should have made my own luck. When someone like you streaks across your life, you stop whatever you're doing and pay attention. I was the numbnuts who didn't.

CHARLIE

(giggles) There was no streaking! I was fully clothed.

DAYTON

You ran up to me to return my football. I remember your eyes. I don't remember what you were wearing. So I'm going to remember it like you were naked.

CHARLIE

You're so full of it. You weren't looking at my eyes.

DAYTON

I am now. They're lovely.

CHARLIE

Sure, with their deep under-eye bags, all these wrinkles...

DAYTON

Screw what the money-driven magazines and movies say! A woman in her forties is like fine wine.

CHARLIE

And you'd know! Because you've had so many women in their forties?

DAYTON

(Feeling sheepish, fixing it) Well... no...but I was waiting for the finest. It took years for you to get this good. In fact, if I can have just one more taste of you, I'll give up Merlot completely.

DAYTON puts his head under the covers and wriggles around. CHARLIE laughs, but suddenly her amused expression turns to deep pleasure.

After a minute, DAYTON comes up for air, literally.

DAYTON (CONT'D)

YES! Young maiden! I am drunk on your Wonderberry Wine!

CHARLIE can't stop giggling now. She feels seen. She feels beautiful.

CHARLIE's phone on the bedside table rings. CHARLIE gives DAYTON an apologetic expression, then reads who it is. When she sees it's JUSTINE, she accepts the call.

INT. BELLEVUE BANQUET HALL - NIGHT

JUSTINE is on her cell phone, her eyes large and intense. There is a brawl behind her.

HARMONY is waving her lit sage sticks at BRIDEZILLA and LUCAS. BRIDEZILLA grabs a red wine from the head table and throws it at HARMONY, but misses and hits her white-haired MOTHER OF THE BRIDE instead.

JUSTINE

Get back here. Your crazy-ass roommate's crashed the wedding.

INT. PRESIDENTIAL SUITE - NIGHT

CHARLIE puts down her phone, grabs her dress off the floor, pulls it over her head. She talks through the dress.

CHARLIE

My voodoo-vampire roommate's here, trying to ruin the wedding.

DAYTON

So let her.

With the dress now pulled over her mussed-up hair, DAYTON reaches over and gently strokes it, trying to convince her to stay in bed.

DAYTON (CONT'D)

We lost so much time. Can't we freeze it for a while...

CHARLIE

(throws his shirt at him) We can't! We have to stop her! I'll lose my job!

DAYTON reluctantly sits up and pulls on his pants. He's only half-zipped, shirt half buttoned, while CHARLIE's at the door, heels in her hands.

CHARLIE (CONT'D)

C'mon!

INT. BELLEVUE HOTEL ELEVATOR - NIGHT

A flustered CHARLIE and DAYTON race out their hotel room door, down the long hallway to an elevator. As the elevator doors open, CHARLIE is fixing her cleavage and DAYTON is tucking his shirt into his pants. They look up to see the REPORTER snapping a photo of their shocked faces.

DAYTON

Hey! don't be a prick!

REPORTER

Too late.

The REPORTER presses a button and closes the elevator. DAYTON pounds on the doors. CHARLIE puts her hand on his to stop him.

CHARLIE

Stairs! We'll get him at the bottom if we hurry.

DAYTON

More running? I'm too old for this shit.

CHARLIE pushes open the door labelled STAIRS and the pair rushes through it.

INT. BELLEVUE BANQUET HALL - NIGHT

Music coming from the banquet hall speakers is ceremonial. CHARLIE and DAYTON rush into the hall looking around for the REPORTER, but they can't find him. Instead they see HARMONY rushing forward from the back of the room to the head table to confront LUCAS and BRIDEZILLA again as they are about to cut their cake. BRIDEZILLA's dress is stained with red wine.

HARMONY

I curse you, Lucas. I curse this union!

BRIDEZILLA puts her hand over LUCAS' to stop him from cutting. The music from the speakers stops. The guests fall silent.

BRIDEZILLA has a wide fake smile for her photographer that she keeps, though her eyes are on HARMONY, who is waving smoking sage and sweetgrass sticks in front of the couple and their cake.

LUCAS

We already talked about this! I didn't send you that text yesterday. It's old! You need to leave!

HARMONY

(holding up her phone, waving the

sticks with other hand) I miss you, baby! You said. Let's get back together! You said!

BRIDEZILLA

(holds up the cake knife in front of LUCAS' horrified face) You said what? When?

A series of flashes. The REPORTER is moving around the scene, snapping away, grinning.

MITCH is ahead of CHARLIE and DAYTON in the crowd. He moves toward BRIDEZILLA, takes the cake knife from her hand and gives her a forced affectionate pat on her back, guiding her away from a stunned LUCAS, away from the head table into a corner of the room.

MITCH

Let's not make this bigger than it has to be. I'm sure there's a logical explanation.

SHARON

Yeah. There's a dim-witted numpty or two at the bloody phone carriers. Bunch of cock-ups.

CHARLIE puts her arm around BRIDEZILLA, gesturing to DAYTON, SEAN, MITCH, JUSTINE and TROY to remove HARMONY from the hall. HARMONY lets them take her away. She seems to be in her own world, waving her smoking sage sticks around the cake and the crowd as she's escorted away.

BRIDEZILLA looks like she's agreeing with MITCH to remain calm. She nods, serene expression on her face, then rushes over to HARMONY, wrestles a sage stick from her hand and whips it at LUCAS' head.

BRIDEZILLA

Nobody puts the Bride in a corner!

LUCAS

(turned on) Oh, Baby, you're hot when you're pissed.

Like a bowling ball to pins, the stick knocks over three lanterns at the head table. The tablecloth is immediately engulfed in flames. Everyone at the table screams and scrambles for cover.

BRIDEZILLA

LUCAS JAMES MAKLEN, if you cheated on me, no one gets out of here alive!

LUCAS

I didn't! I swear, I texted her six months back! When we were on a break!

BRIDEZILLA

So that's what it's called now?

BRIDEZILLA is enraged, but has a slight smirk, oddly turned on knowing her groom likes her in this state. She whips off her shoes and knocks down the other lanterns, meanwhile, the head table is on fire and the flames are encroaching on all the other tables. The guests are screaming and attempting to leave the hall, but they're tripping on each other as they try to avoid new flames.

MITCH pulls a fire extinguisher off the wall and aims it at the head table, but discovers it's empty. CHARLIE calls 911.

CHARLIE

(shouting into cell) No! The sprinkler system isn't coming on!

DAYTON rushes to tackle BRIDEZILLA to stop her from doing any more harm.

BRIDEZILLA falls to the ground and seems calm again, only to sit up, struggle out of his grasp and punch DAYTON firmly on the chin. He's bloody and shaken, lying on the floor. BRIDEZILLA gets up and wanders off to the head table, unsteady on her feet.

BRIDEZILLA

This fucking cake cost us $600, I'm not going anywhere without tasting some.

She's in shock, not logical anymore. She's shoving wedding cake into her mouth with her hands, stress-eating.

DAYTON looks at MITCH who has HARMONY in his grasp. She's staring at all the flames and chanting, totally orgasmic over them.

DAYTON

Bonkers. Everyone's gone bonkers.

The curtains on the stage where DAYTON and SEAN played suddenly go up in flames.

DAYTON (CONT'D)

And I thought the smoldering sweetgrass was going to be a problem.

MITCH

(Shouts) Everyone outside NOW!

MITCH pulls the alarm on the wall and it sounds. He guides HARMONY out of the hall with one arm, using the other arm in a sweeping movement like a cross walk guard with a whistle to usher the guests out of the hall. Guests that hadn't been heading for the doors do so now. It's pandemonium.

With smoke getting thicker, everyone starts to leave, screaming and coughing. CHARLIE looks behind her shoulder and notices BRIDEZILLA fainting to the floor. She rushes back and checks her vitals. She discovers she's choking on cake.

CHARLIE

Help! A little help here!

Through the smoke and over the alarm and panic, it seems no one can see or hear her. CHARLIE pulls BRIDEZILLA up enough to get her arms around her chest and performs the Heimlich.

CHARLIE (CONT'D)

You're not going to die today, bitch.

BRIDEZILLA spits out a chunk of cake and starts gasping for air. She hugs CHARLIE, who's both laughing and coughing. BRIDEZILLA looks around, sees the place is on fire, gets up and stumbles out of the hall, not looking back. CHARLIE's eyes widen. She's gasping for air as she crawls on the floor towards the exit.

Looking less and less alert, CHARLIE reaches out for someone...but no one is there. Her head falls to the floor where she lays, seemingly lifeless.

INT. BELLEVUE LOBBY - NIGHT

It's utter chaos. Firefighters are entering the lobby and ushering the last of the guests out the doors. The CHIEF FIREFIGHTER and OFFICER are talking with MITCH and HARMONY in a corner; the OFFICER puts handcuffs on a dazed and confused HARMONY and ushers her out the hotel's glass doors to the police car parked in the front.

LUCAS kisses BRIDEZILLA, who's been in a corner catching her breath, then lifts her up in her massive, destroyed gown and carries her out the doors.

EXT. ENTRANCE TO BELLEVUE HOTEL - NIGHT

As LUCAS comes through the revolving doors in slow motion, he looks like the hero in every movie, carrying the damsel out of the flames. HARMONY is being put into the back of a police cruiser. She looks over her shoulder and rolls her eyes dramatically.

HARMONY

Cringey. He never let me be a feminist anyway. Fuck him.

Just as she says this, LUCAS gets stuck in the revolving doors and BRIDEZILLA is squished like a hamster in its plastic sphere.

HARMONY gets her last laugh; she's chuckling in the back of the cruiser.

BRIDEZILLA

Lucas! What have you done?

INT. BELLVUE HOTEL LOBBY - NIGHT

It's a wet snow on a dark night. A distraught DAYTON comes storming out of the double doors of the Banquet hall, a lifeless-looking

CHARLIE in his arms. There's no cheesy slow motion this time, but his bulging arm muscles and chest take up most of the screen. He is not just a rockstar, now he's a superhero.

DAYTON circles through the hotel doors which have been cleared of BRIDEZILLA, who is in the back of an ambulance screaming insults at an ambulance attendant.

EXT. BELLEVUE HOTEL ENTRANCE - NIGHT

DAYTON rushes to the ambulance parked behind the one with BRIDEZILLA in it.

DAYTON

You've gotta help me! She isn't breathing!

Two FIRST RESPONDERS rush to take CHARLIE from DAYTON's arms and start performing CPR on her.

As they continue working on her, wedding guests are still rushing across the street to safety. They end up standing and gaping at the FIRST RESPONDERS and the now-burning lobby. Some PASSERSBY approach the victims and wrap blankets around their shoulders.

Firefighters pull a hose into the building as the circle of people huddled around CHARLIE keep trying to save her life.

It's reminiscent of the first scene when CHARLIE was alone in a parking lot, only now DAYTON is afraid and miserable, standing on wet pavement alone under a lamplight, getting soaked in the sleet.

INT. NEW YORK HOSPITAL - EARLY MORNING

DAYTON paces a waiting room where several other waiting people are unsuccessfully trying to sleep on the chairs, including SHARON,

JUSTINE and their new love interests. An ER
DOCTOR enters the room. DAYTON stops
pacing, frozen in fear.

ER DOCTOR

You're waiting on Ms. Charlene James?

DAYTON

(nods) Is she okay?

ER DOCTOR

She inhaled a lot of smoke, but someone got her
out in time.

Hearing it's good news, SHARON, MITCH,
JUSTINE and TROY join DAYTON in
standing.

SHARON

It was this bloke. He's the hero.

DAYTON

No I'm not. Charlie saved the bride and got
herself out. I just carried her half way.

SHARON

(swooning) You carried her half way! Bloody romantic!

DAYTON

(shrugs) When you love someone you meet them half way.

JUSTINE and SHARON give each other a wide-eyed, impressed look. DAYTON is a keeper.

JUSTINE

Charlie can take care of herself. I've seen her in trouble before, but this one was a close call. Thank God she made it.

MITCH AND SHARON

(to the doctor) Can we see her?

ER DOCTOR

She's on oxygen, so don't make her talk.

JUSTINE

(pulls a tablet out of her bag) We won't. We'll use my tablet.

ER DOCTOR

She's one lucky lady to have you all pulling for her. You can go in two at a time. I want to keep her under observation another 24 hours.

INT. CHARLIE'S CURTAINED OFF HOSPITAL BED - EARLY MORNING

DAYTON pulls the curtain to enter, pulling it again for privacy. He smiles at CHARLIE and takes her hand. She's in an oxygen mask and looks exhausted.

CHARLIE

You saved me.

DAYTON

Shhh. Don't waste your energy.

CHARLIE

But...

DAYTON

We have forever to talk.

He takes her other hand so he's holding them
both.

DAYTON (CONT'D)

Charlie. You were always going to be okay.
You're a survivor. I just reminded you that
you've got reasons to stick around.

CHARLIE beams at him and squeezes his
hands.

DAYTON (CONT'D)

Let's get a place. Not my place or yours, one we
pick together. It'd have to be smaller...I'm living
on savings now. Not sure when my next gig will
be...

CHARLIE

(Takes off her mask) Oh sweetie, I made a promise to my friends, to move in with them, I should stand by my girlfriends.

SHARON and JUSTINE have been listening and they rip open the curtain and come inside.

SHARON

Sex on a pogo stick wants to move in with you and you're choosing us?

CHARLIE

(chuckles, starts to cough, puts mask back on) We chose each other first!

JUSTINE

Sharon, don't make her talk! But seriously, girl, did you hit your head in that fire?

CHARLIE

(whispers) You'd be okay with it...?

JUSTINE holds out her hand. It has a candy ring pop jewel on it.

JUSTINE

TROY wants to get hitched.

SHARON

(snickers) Boy Toy TROY? Did you mention you're still married?

JUSTINE

Now wait, older men rob the cradle all the time, don't you go there with me! Besides, we're waiting a year, at least. So don't be judging.

CHARLIE

No judging! We always promised each other! We are a zero-judgment zone! (coughs)

SHARON

Just don't want you to get hurt.

JUSTINE

I appreciate that, but from where I'm standing,

looks like you're already in the fast lane with Manager Mitch.

SHARON

(smirks) He *did* ask me to move in

with him...

CHARLIE's eyes grow wide. She claps her hands in excitement.

DAYTON

Sounds like you two are otherwise occupicd. So we're good?

SHARON

You're good.

JUSTINE

Do it. We're behind you! And we can have a house warming party that doesn't involve fire.

CHARLIE holds her mask, inhales more oxygen, then starts to speak to DAYTON.

JUSTINE (CONT'D)

Wait, save your breath sweetie. Here.

JUSTINE hands her friend the tablet.

CHARLIE types a phrase in the Notes section and holds it up for DAYTON to read:

CHARLIE

I CANNOT WAIT TO LIVE WITH YOU

Before DAYTON can respond, CHELSEA, a thin, glamorous blonde woman, 25, in a tight dress, heels and black shades rips open the curtain and enters, taking up the space of three people and making JUSTINE lose her balance.

DAYTON

CHELSEA! What are you doing here?

CHELSEA takes off her shades and holds up a headline story in the New York Post. It has the photo, front and centre, taken at the hotel of a shocked looking, half-dressed CHARLIE and DAYTON tucking his shirt into his pants at the elevator. It reads:

DAYTON HILL DISASTER GIG!

CHELSEA

Lover, what have you done? I leave you for one night and your reputation's down the toilet! It's the headline, and all over social media. We have to fix this.

CHARLIE

(Holds up Tablet) LOVER?

DAYTON ignores CHELSEA and squeezes CHARLIE's hands tighter.

DAYTON

It's not what you think. You know me.

CHARLIE rips off her mask.

CHARLIE

I know you? I KNOW you? Apparently not, since you have another LOVER I've never heard about!

JUSTINE

I knew about her. Thought you did too. She was his date for last year's Grammys...

CHELSEA puts her hands on her hips and clears her throat.

CHELSEA

Excuse me. It was the AMAs. Last fall. I was sick for the Grammy's or he'd have asked me...

DAYTON

How do you come up with these lies? She's not my girlfriend.

CHELSEA

(clears throat before reading paper out loud)
DAYTON HILL is pictured half naked with
hotel employee CHARLENE JAMES. Where
was *his girlfriend* CHELSEA FLEM?

DAYTON

Girlfriend, according to the press! Charlie, trust
me. I haven't even seen her since last fall.

CHELSEA rubs her hand on DAYTON's chest.

CHELSEA

Really. Darling. Now who's lying. You've seen
all of me, on your phone...

DAYTON

She sends me pictures. I don't open them!

CHARLIE's face grows red and her eyes fill
with tears. She writes furiously on her tablet,
then holds it up for DAYTON to read.

CHARLIE

GET. OUT.

DAYTON (CONT'D)

Charlie, I'd never intentionally hurt you! My
concerts weren't selling out. My old label and
manager screwed me over. I've had to dip into
my savings. I'm over the hill in the music biz
now.

SHARON

Surely you can always sell music?

DAYTON shrugs.

DAYTON

It's all about social media presence, streaming,
things I'm learning, but I'm not at the top of my
game. People pay to see 20-year-old rappers, not
40-year-old has-beens.

CHELSEA is getting bored. She's fixing her lipstick in a little compact mirror.

CHELSEA

Um, hello. What does this have to do with ME?

CHARLIE

(GROANS)

DAYTON

Whirl-a-girl, please, trust me! My publicist thought this up. He thought it would help me sell tickets if I showed off a young girlfriend on my arm when I'm out in public. I fought with him, but finally agreed to a couple dates...

CHARLIE rolls her eyes, but they are brimming with tears. She types on the tablet and turns it around:

CHARLIE

PLEASE JUST LEAVE.

JUSTINE scowls at DAYTON and starts to show him out of the curtained area.

JUSTINE

So, now you're a two-timing has-been? And how's that working for you? 'Cause it doesn't work for me, or my friend. Goodbye, Dayton. She wrote you off.

MITCH enters the curtained room and watches a slumpy shouldered DAYTON leaving and a clingy, whiny CHELSEA chasing after him. But MITCH is not really paying attention, he's distracted and gathering the courage to speak to CHARLIE.

MITCH

Charlie. It's not me, okay, it's head office. I'm canned, and so are you.

He glances at SHARON before he lowers his head. She grimaces.

SHARON

That's total shite! Let me talk to them! I'll set them straight!

CHARLIE lowers her oxygen mask and whispers.

CHARLIE

Sharon, stop, it's fine. Really, it's fine.

SHARON

How is this ballsed-up mess fine?

CHARLIE

Because I realized something today.

JUSTINE

What is it honey?

CHARLIE finds energy to whisper somewhat louder, although she sounds breathless, obviously still needing the oxygen.

CHARLIE

I fucking hate weddings.

EXT. HOSPITAL PATIENT LOADING
DOCK AREA - THE NEXT DAY

The snow has melted; it's looking more like an
early spring. MITCH is walking CHARLIE to
his car, where JUSTINE and SHARON are in
the back waiting for them. As he opens the
passenger door for her, SHARON gets out of the
car and offers her other hand to steady her.

SHARON

Watch your step. I know you think

you can do everything...

CHARLIE

Nah, I know I can't. I get everything wrong.

MITCH

Hey hey, none of that talk here. Let's get you
home to my place to rest.

CHARLIE

Thank you boss.

MITCH starts to correct her, but then doesn't.
Before CHARLIE gets in the passenger seat,
BRIDEZILLA appears behind them in a
wheelchair, being wheeled to her car by
LUCAS.

BRIDEZILLA

You were on observation too huh? Wasn't the
tapioca pudding disgusting?

CHARLIE turns to look at them.

CHARLIE

Wow! You two patched things up fast!

BRIDEZILLA

Well, he IS the father of my baby.

She gets teary and taps her belly, which has a
barely visible bump. LUCAS looks
uncomfortable and gives CHARLIE a shrug.

LUCAS

The police say we can fight the hotel chain's charges against her.

He pauses to look down at his bride, who's looking at CHARLIE.

MITCH

Really? On what grounds?

LUCAS   **BRIDEZILLA**

Temporary insanity.   It wasn't my fault!

BRIDEZILLA realizes they were speaking at the same time and wants to make sure she gets the last word.

BRIDEZILLA

That woman trespassed and crashed my wedding! I hope she does some hard time! It wasn't my fault!

MITCH and SHARON exchange a glance. CHARLIE sighs and starts to get in the car again.

CHARLIE

Well, good luck with that.

BRIDEZILLA

Wait! We want to throw this massive

gender reveal party in five months! So we were

thinking...

CHARLIE cuts her off. LUCAS is clenching the handles of BRIDEZILLA's wheelchair, looking down at his feet.

CHARLIE

Oh, no...no.

BRIDEZILLA

Could you, like, organize it? I mean not at the hotel obviously. In our backyard? So we can have blue fireworks?

JUSTINE

You sure fire's the way to go, folks?

CHARLIE gets in the car.

CHARLIE

Hell to the no.

She slams her door.

BRIDEZILLA

But...but...you owe me! All of you!

She starts throwing a tantrum in her wheelchair. LUCAS rushes around the front, bends down and takes her hands, strokes her hair, trying to calm her.

MITCH and SHARON get in the car quick. MITCH pulls the car away.

INT - MITCH'S CAR - DAY

CHARLIE

Love is strange.

MITCH AND SHARON

You don't have to tell us.

JUSTINE

Been there, done that, got the t- shirt.

CHARLIE

Yet we keep trying, again and again.

SHARON

It should be called temporary insanity.

JUSTINE

You got that right.

MITCH

You three are depressing. I'm stopping for sundaes.

He pulls over to a place called ICE CREAM HUT. SHARON's face lights up as she looks at the sign, then back at MITCH.

SHARON

You sure know how to comfort a woman! I think I'll keep you.

INT. NEW YORK MUSIC BOOKING AGENCY OFFICE - DAY

A clean, professional looking office with big windows, roomy enough for a sofa and a couple of chairs in it. Music concert posters and framed gold discs adorn the walls, several of them Dayton's. Dayton's publicist J.J., now 65 and bald, has his legs up on his own desk and is slurping away at a big cola in a cup with a straw, scrolling his phone. DAYTON storms into the office without knocking. CHELSEA isn't far behind him and doesn't look at all pleased to still be trailing after him in her dress and heels. He throws a newspaper onto the desk.

DAYTON

J.J. Was it you?

J.J.

Good morning to you too.

DAYTON

No more B.S! Did you call in the story about my night with Charlie to the press?

J.J.

So what if I did? You're no spring chicken anymore, Dayton.

DAYTON

Yeah, look in the mirror!

J.J. frowns but keeps speaking.

J.J.

Ahem. You need buzz. Buzz sells

tickets. We've been through this.

DAYTON

I don't care about selling seats in big stadiums anymore. I've wasted too much time on that.

J.J.

Are you saying you regret your career?

DAYTON

I'm saying my priorities have changed. And why did you have to drag Charlie into any of this? I only went out with Chelsea twice.

CHELSEA is sick of standing and lies down quite seductively on the couch, trying to convince DAYTON one more time.

CHELSEA

It would have been more times if you'd only opened my photos.

DAYTON

Chelsea, please. Enough! I made it clear I'm not interested.

CHELSEA sits up, pouting.

CHELSEA

Yea but J.J. paid me till the end of the summer...

J.J.

Chelsea, that was between us.

J.J. stands up, glaring at CHELSEA. DAYTON walks closer to J.J. like he wants to hit him, but pulls back and stops himself.

DAYTON

Jesus, J.J.! What did you do? I can get my own dates!

J.J.

Can you though? You hit your 40s and started spending a lot of nights moping alone at home. I thought you needed some help.

DAYTON

First, you didn't want me to have a girlfriend. Now you do? Guess what J.J.? I don't need your sneaky, misguided help. I'm in love!

J.J. laughs in his face.

J.J.

You're in love? At your age?

DAYTON

Yes, on cloud nine, head over heels, till death do us part love! I think I've been in love with her all my life. I just didn't realize it till now. (pauses, softer) And I've probably lost her forever.

J.J.

Well goody goody for you! But I book all the concert halls!

DAYTON

It's a new world J.J.! I can change. I can try live streaming. Book online shows. I'm done with your games. You're fired.

J.J. puts his hands on his friend's shoulders, attempting a manly hug.

J.J.

Aw, come on, Kid! Kid!

DAYTON pushes him away and starts to leave.

DAYTON

I'm not a kid anymore.

DAYTON storms out of the office, not looking back.

CHELSEA doesn't follow DAYTON, she puts her arms around J.J.'s neck, cozies up and looks up at him.

CHELSEA

So, like, will I still get my free Brazilian bum cream?

INT. A SMALL THREE-BEDROOM NEW YORK APARTMENT - **TWO WEEKS LATER** - DAY

JUSTINE and SHARON are sitting close together on the middle of the wooden floor, surrounded by boxes. They're unpacking one box each, but every time SHARON takes something out of hers, JUSTINE makes a disgusted face, takes it from her hand and tosses it in the garbage pail beside her. SHARON is trying to be a good roommate, but after this happens twice, the third time, SHARON pushes back.

SHARON takes an old orange, black and yellow 3-D- macramé elephant wall-hanging out of the garbage pail, gets up, and holds it up on the wall. It's the ugliest, creepiest looking elephant you can imagine.

SHARON

It has character!

JUSTINE

It has dust mites.

SHARON

It was me grandmothers.

JUSTINE stands, her mouth agape.

JUSTINE

So it was buried with her and you dug it up?

Sharon laughs at that, but still tries the hanging
on another wall.

SHARON

What? You'd think with your African roots...

JUSTINE isn't offended but lets on that she is.

JUSTINE

Ohhhh don't play the black card with me, just to
get your ugly ass shit on our walls.

SHARON laughs, takes the hanging down,
drops it on the sofa and playfully hip checks her
friend.

SHARON

Fine. I'm tired. Tea?

JUSTINE stops pulling items out of her box and smiles up at SHARON.

JUSTINE

That we can agree on.

SHARON

Early grey?

JUSTINE

You should know it. You have lots of them on that head of yours.

SHARON has gone to the kitchen and put on the kettle, but she pokes her head around the doorframe.

SHARON

Bitch! I embrace my all-natural roots and you

try to embarrass me for it. The Sisterhood is a LIE!

The door opens just as SHARON is shouting that last line.

CHARLIE

What the Shatner, are you two at it again?

JUSTINE

Just trying to keep each other awake.

CHARLIE, in a t-shirt, jean jacket and leggings, takes off her runners and sets a grocery bag down on the floor beside the door.

CHARLIE

I can't believe you're still not done unpacking. I was done a week ago.

SHARON comes from the kitchen, gives CHARLIE a tight hug, then collects the grocery bag.

SHARON

You were heartbroken. People have written entire operas thanks to heartbreak.

CHARLIE

Super. And all I did was arrange my socks by color.

JUSTINE

Sit with us. You've been avoiding us.

CHARLIE

Have not. I'm busy! I'm trying to find a new job! Do you know how many hotels have heard of the Dayton Hill disaster gig and think it's all my fault?

SHARON pokes her head around the kitchen doorframe again, offering her friend an empathetic look.

SHARON

Um. All of them?

CHARLIE

Pretty much!

JUSTINE

Honey, we know that, but you're also trying to shove your pain under the carpet.

CHARLIE shakes her head defiantly.

CHARLIE

I see no carpets here. I see only wood floors.
She turns and starts to walk to her room.

JUSTINE

Just sit with us a second!

CHARLIE sighs and reluctantly comes to sit on the small sofa beside JUSTINE. SHARON hands both ladies a cup of tea, then goes to the kitchen to get her own cup.

JUSTINE (CONT'D)

Thanks sweetie.

SHARON returns and sits on the floor. JUSTINE and CHARLIE are squished together on the small sofa.

They all sip their tea quietly, looking around at the almost unfurnished apartment and unopened boxes. It's uncomfortable.

CHARLIE finally breaks the silence.

CHARLIE

This is perfect, right? This is what we always wanted. The three amigos! Sharing a home.

Everyone is forcing a smile.

JUSTINE

Perfect. Oh, yeah, for sure. We didn't want to rush into anything with Troy or Mitch. This is perfect.

SHARON's smile fades.

SHARON

Perfect? Furniture would be good.

JUSTIN

Utensils would be better. Eating that fusilli with our hands last night because YOU keep forgetting to buy us forks was a low point.

SHARON

Would you stop being such a buzz kill. I had to save up. I'll buy us some tomorrow.

JUSTINE

Maybe if you didn't keep buying sex toys off the internet we'd have money for our forking forks!

SHARON stands up.

SHARON

I did nothing of the sort!

JUSTINE gets up in a huff and grabs an unopened, rectangular box off the floor.

JUSTINE

You did so. Amazon delivered it this morning when you were still snoring.

SHARON

You opened my mail!

JUSTINE

NO. I asked what our notifications were and Alexa announced you bought a big yellow dildo.

SHARON

WELL. I can't have Mitch over here, you'd all listen in!

JUSTINE

Yeah right! We'd fall asleep from boredom. Bring it! I have insomnia.

CHARLIE

Enough! You two are driving me NUTSO!

JUSTINE

We're driving YOU nuts? All you do is whine

about Dayton, 24-7. I'm eating my morning fruit salad, you're all, Oh, Dayton loved strawberries! I'm watching American Idol and you're all, Dayton could totally host this show!

SHARON

You do say his name ALL the time. You draw it out, let it linger on your tongue. You'd think you belonged with him or something.

She turns to stare at CHARLIE. It's a long silent stare.

CHARLIE

He had a GIRLFRIEND.

JUSTINE

Hardly! It was just for show.

SHARON

I know it stung, but we thought you'd forgive him sooner...

CHARLIE

What? I thought you two were on my side.
Together forever!

JUSTINE

Honey. We're always on your side. But you're
fucking miserable.

SHARON looks at JUSTINE and nods.

SHARON

We agree on something.

JUSTINE

We do. (pauses) We do?

SHARON

There's loyalty, and then there's plain old
stubbornness and getting in your own way.

CHARLIE

My own way? You think I made a mistake?

Before they answer, she puts down her tea and
starts sobbing into her hands.

SHARON

Maybe. We all have.

SHARON takes CHARLIE'S long strand of hair at the front of her face and tucks it behind her ear, then lovingly fixes her hair back into a ponytail.

SHARON (CONT'D)

But the best thing about being in our 40s is we've made enough mistakes now to know that they force us to grow. And we can fix them.

JUSTINE

Uh... Most of the time. I couldn't fix your Wonder Woman coffee mug.

SHARON

You fucking broke my Wonder Woman mug?

The two glare at one another in silence, but then CHARLIE sniffles, blows her nose.

CHARLIE

You're both right. I belong with him.

CHARLIE comes to a realization and starts laughing hysterically.

CHARLIE (CONT'D)

Oh no. No. No... I can't leave. There's the lease. Plus, if I leave, you guys are gonna kill each other!

JUSTINE reaches for her purse that's beside the sofa and pulls out a rental agreement document. She shows it to CHARLIE.

JUSTINE

Still unsigned. The landlord is in Florida, very laissez-faire. I'm sure you can get out of it.

SHARON

I never signed it either. Mitch's place is gorgeous! I just didn't want to ditch my besties for a man. I love you both so much!

JUSTINE

Love you too. But sometimes love means separate apartments.

SHARON laughs and nods. JUSTINE wipes CHARLIE's tears and the three of them have a group hug. They laugh together, huddled on the small sofa.

CHARLIE

You know what this means?

JUSTINE

I can dance in my underwear to *What A Feeling* without you two watching?

SHARON

You like it when we watch.

CHARLIE

It means I'm going to have to admit to Dayton that I was wrong.

JUSTINE

You've got this. Just whatever you do, don't text the apology.

EXT. ATLANTIC BEACH PARK, RHODE ISLAND, TWO DAYS LATER

It's a gorgeous early spring day. The Ferris wheel is full of laughing teenagers. The park has an upbeat feeling to it, with music playing and diverse groups of friends greeting one another with smiles and hugs.

DAYTON is staring at his phone, squinting, looking frustrated.

A younger PARK GOER standing beside him studies the phone. It's on an app with this title which we clearly see:

REAL LIFE HIDE AND SEEK

The PARK GOER studies it closer, smiles, nods, then starts pointing over to where CHARLIE is standing.

CHARLIE is leaning her back up against a colorful game booth filled with stuffed elephants, seals and penguins.

CHARLIE

You finally found me.

DAYTON holds up his phone in the air, and celebrates the win. He does an adorable little celebratory booty shaking dance, then picks her up and swings her around in his arms. After a few seconds he puts her down and puts his arms on her shoulders.

DAYTON

I absolutely love the games you have us play, but I couldn't find my fucking prescription sunglasses anywhere, so I've had to ask complete strangers to help me read subway signs and my phone all morning. By the way, Frank and Carrie from Manhattan are having us for dinner next week.

CHARLIE

Ha. And I thought I was getting old!

DAYTON

Hey hey, you invited me here, do you want me back or not?

CHARLIE

Of course. I thought you'd never come.

DAYTON

Just took me 21 years. But now you're stuck with me, Whirl-a-Girl.

CHARLIE

I'll gladly stick, as long as we never keep secrets. I'm sorry I didn't trust you.

He gives her a kiss.

DAYTON

No secrets. I'll always check that you like my fake girlfriends.

CHARLIE

Not funny!

DAYTON

Hey, let me try to win you one of these. You want an elephant?

CHARLIE

Hmm...elephants are big (chuckles) but I'll take a penguin. They mate for life.

DAYTON chuckles with her.

DAYTON

Really? I'm sure some try on the rock star life first.

CHARLIE

Oh yes, but rock star penguins always see the error of their ways.

DAYTON pays the BOOTH LADY ten dollars and takes the balls she gives him.

DAYTON

What about the clever but stubborn girl penguins? Do they, too, see the...error of their ways?

He winds up to throw a ball at the target, but CHARLIE tickles him under both armpits from behind and he misses.

CHARLIE

They say shut up, I asked you here, didn't I?

DAYTON

Fair enough. Now stop tickling me or you'll get the big old elephant instead.

CHARLIE

Mmmmmmm. I think I might.

They're laughing hard, kissing one another, and the BOOTH LADY is just rolling her eyes.

INT. CHARLIE AND DAYTON'S NEW YORK APARTMENT BUILDING - DAY

SUBTITLE: ONE MONTH LATER

DAYTON and CHARLIE leave a modestly-sized and decorated apartment together, both giving kisses to their two cats before shutting the door. They stop to get the mail in the lobby. CHARLIE hands DAYTON three letters from their box, he smiles, folds them, puts them in his back pocket.

CHARLIE

(Giggles) We're going to need a PO box. Your friends don't send you DMs? Or emails?

DAYTON

Oh, we both know how those take six months to get to me. I trust snail mail more. Old reliable.

CHARLIE

(laughs and wraps her arms around him) You're my old reliable!

DAYTON

You too. As long as you're not driving.

Priscilla the car is parked on the street in front of them, bright and sparkly, eyelashes intact, with a new paint job. CHARLIE gives DAYTON a playful shove as they laugh together. They walk down their steps and off along the sidewalk hand in hand, watching spring come to life in their community.

EXT. FRONT OF CHARLIE AND DAYTON'S NEW YORK APARTMENT BUILDING - DAY

CHARLIE and DAYTON are walking around their community, content and soaking in the Spring weather, flower boxes, kids playing hop scotch, people on their balconies. CHARLIE has very little makeup on and her blonde-grey hair is flowing down across her shoulders. She is confident and rocking Forty.

EXT. NEW YORK ALLEY - THAT SAME MORNING - DAY

Previously homeless JOSH is wearing new jeans and a clean t- shirt. He's standing on a ladder, leaning over to paint a colorful mural of birds on the alley wall. There are two other PAINTERS working with him.

CHARLIE

Hey! Josh! Wow, that's beautiful. You've found work again! How? What happened?

JOSH pulls back from the wall, paintbrush in hand, and waves it at her. The paint flies onto his t-shirt, and he laughs, then grins at her. He starts to climb down as he speaks.

JOSH

Wifi at the warming centre. Finally received the text I needed. It got delayed, but it finally got to me.

A beautiful woman, NORA, 35, comes around the corner with bags of take-out food and some painting supplies in her hands. She smiles at JOSH with love. He steps off the last step of the ladder and greets her with a kiss, then nods to CHARLIE and DAYTON.

JOSH (CONT'D)

Charlie, this is my Nora.

CHARLIE smiles and shakes NORA's hand. DAYTON shakes both JOSH's and NORA's hands.

CHARLIE

And this is my Dayton. I'm so happy things worked out for you.

JOSH

Better late than never.

NORA

We met years ago while working at the Audubon society. We were separated for a while, but Josh found his way back to me.

Her love for JOSH is evident when she looks at him.

JOSH

The mural represents endangered birds.

CHARLIE and DAYTON admire the mural.

JOSH (CONT'D)

Do you like painting? They're still hiring for the summer.

CHARLIE

I don't know, but lately, I like to try new things. Change can be good.

DAYTON looks down at CHARLIE and pulls her into his side for a cuddle, and they share a knowing glance.

NORA

The society needs new people on the board too. Take my card. Give me a call!

She hands CHARLIE her card and CHARLIE studies it, her smile growing wider.

CHARLIE

Thanks! I think I'll do that.

EXT. CENTRAL PARK - MAY - DAY

A seabird like the gannet at the start of the film soars above central park to an uplifting song that conjures feelings about lasting friendship.

DAYTON and CHARLIE are walking hand in hand into a green and blossoming Central Park.

The couple approaches JUSTINE, TROY, MITCH and SHARON who are playing frisbee.

When JUSTINE tackles TROY to try to get the frisbee, they fall to the ground laughing. JUSTINE is on her back, unable to get up, but laughing. CHARLIE runs over, laughing, and offers JUSTINE her hand to help her up.

SHARON motions for the ladies to go over to a picnic table, and they all start setting up a picnic for the group of friends.

CUT TO

As the song continues, footage of the same couples from the street and café last VALENTINES DAY, greeting one another at the café with hugs and kisses, playing sports and having picnics in Central Park.

CHARLIE (V.O.)

Society still makes me feel obsolete; like I'm walking around with a Best Before date stamped on my forehead. But I've found my place in the world, and I'll never be invisible to this loyal group of friends. I'm living my Best After.

Some of the people in the park are with the same person; others are with someone new. None are scrolling their phones, they're laughing, kissing, enjoying New York together on a perfect Spring day.

Technology can't mess with love. At least not today.

And as the credits roll...DAYTON's newest hit song BEST BEFORE plays...

DAYTON (V.O. SINGING)

Don't Hey, Boomer me,

Or hang my Grad year on the tree.

I don't do labels,
legends or fables.
But I'll still spin you 'round

the ol' dance floor

When you age like fine wine

There's no best before.

INT. CHARLIE AND DAYTON'S NYC
APARTMENT - NIGHT

DAYTON is singing the rest of the song, sitting
at his computer, doing a livestream show for
thousands of viewers. We can see the viewer
number in the corner of his computer screen,
and him strumming his guitar, singing the
catchy tune with a grin on his face.

CHARLIE is dancing with her girlfriends
JUSTINE and SHARON. They're beautiful
because they're happy in their own skin.

There's a dance party in their small living room.
MITCH dips SHARON, TROY does a
breakdancing head-spin on the floor and then
just lies there flat on his back, exhausted, even

at his young age. JUSTINE mocks him before helping him up. Everyone's laughing and having the fantastic party they wanted to have before the hotel lit up on fire.

As the final credits roll, there's one little wink left. The song fades enough for the clear sound of a knock on the door. SHARON rushes to open the door first. CHARLIE is right behind her, dancing with DAYTON. She sees HARMONY and stops dancing.

HARMONY

Party People! I got out after three months on good behavior! Wines of any kind?

HARMONY holds up a bottle of red wine in one hand and a bottle of white in the other. She's now wearing a whole new 1950s vibe outfit, with her hair in a high ponytail, a hot pink poodle skirt and a light pink cardigan. But even with the goody-two-shoes outfit, her makeup and expression suggest she is someone they all need to be very afraid of.

We see the HOTEL FRONT DESK CLERK behind her, holding a silver platter of a variety of cheeses, looking at HARMONY lovingly.

SHARON

Crikey!

CHARLIE

HELL NO!

CHARLIE starts to slam the door, but DAYTON catches it with his hand. He peers out the door and surveys the cheeses.

DAYTON

Wait, is that the good Gouda?

CHARLIE

The good Gouda? What is wrong with you?

She slams the door.

THE END.

Thanks for Reading!

Please leave a star rating and quick review on Amazon, Goodreads and Bookbub to help more people discover this book. To read Heather's other screenplay *The Friends I've Never Met* and her novels and poetry books, please visit her Shor page:

http://Shor.by/HGS

Sign up there with one click for the Heather Grace Stewart Books Club. You'll get a free ebook and be entered in her contests and you'll be the first to learn about her exclusive book bargains and new releases. All of Heather's social media links are at the bottom of her Shor page.

www.ingramcontent.com/pod-product-compliance
Lightning Source LLC
Chambersburg PA
CBHW061821040426
42447CB00012B/2759